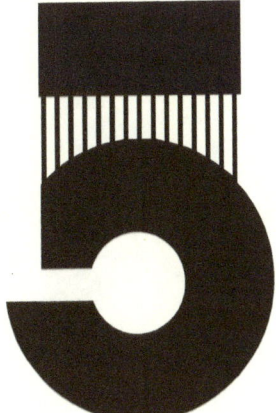 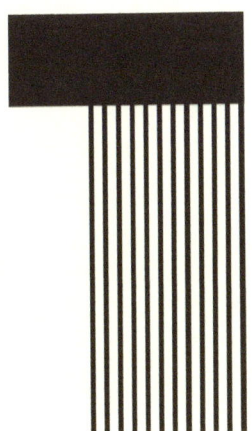

A Division of Groom Lake, Inc.

New York | Los Angeles

Darren Callahan's

BEAUTIFUL WOMEN IN TERRIBLE TROUBLE

Three Plays About Hollywood

Library of Congress information:

Callahan, Darren, 1969-

Beautiful Women in Terrible Trouble – 1st ed. in the United States of America

p. cm.

ISBN 1502306506

Published by 51Works, 51 Bleecker Street, New York, New York, 10012 USA and 931 South Broadway, Los Angeles, California 90015

Printed in the United States of America

10 9 8 7 6 5 4 3 2 1

The Playwright

Darren Callahan has written drama for the BBC, SyFy Channel, National Public Radio, and Radio Pacifica New York. Stage plays include *The White Airplane* and *Horror Academy*, both published by Polarity Books, *The Double Negative*, *Mad Scientist Double Feature* (which includes the plays *Mass Grave* and *Sub-Genre*), and *Beautiful Women in Terrible Trouble* (which includes *Witness to An Accident*, *Desperate Dolls*, and *Sources*.) Novels include *The Audrey Green Chronicles* trilogy, *City of Human Remains*, and *The Vanishing of Archie Gray*. Screenplays include *Documentia*, *Nerves*, *Summer of Ghosts*, and *The Battle for Carlyle*. He is writer, director, and composer of the film *Under the Table*. Also a musician, he has released many records, including film soundtracks, on various labels. His website is darrencallahan.com.

The Concept

Beautiful Women in Terrible Trouble is the 'umbrella' title for three separate, full-length plays: *Witness to an Accident*, *Desperate Dolls*, and *Sources*. They're not sequels, they don't share characters, but together they create a bonded narrative — a 'world' — with thematic similarities and stylistic cohesion. If you see or read all three plays, it forms a whole much greater than the sum of the parts.

Plays about movies would seem to be at odds, but not here. These pieces are fully theatrical and built to be produced by companies of various sizes, means, and resources. To sustain an atmosphere for six hours requires focus and uniformity, as well as talent. Challenging texts require engagement from performers and audiences, and these plays are at the top of their game.

Witness to an Accident is big studios, split personalities, and Hollywood mental homes; *Desperate Dolls* is independent films, hypnosis, and auditions gone wrong; *Sources* is snuff films, amnesia, and ingénues. Each play goes deeper into the darkest side of Tinseltown — a sort of 'Hollywood Babylon' for the modern audience. These can be characterized as thrillers, or intense dramas, with heavy style and the right amount of substance to keep things grounded. Fundamentally, these are horror plays, as Darren Callahan's horror fans expect, but these also include mystery, noir, and Italian Giallo.

The shows were intended as a 'cross-town classic' — a partnership between different ensembles, different casts, different directors, and different locations (even experimental spaces). Patrons could buy a ticket to one show, but it is best under a festival pass for all three plays at a bundled price. It's a large commitment — both for audiences and for theatres. It requires separate companies to commit to produce the plays concurrently or consecutively. And to be ready for controversy.

Let's not forget the lurid appeal of the subject matter. These plays are *sexy* — almost wickedly so. They're not porn, but they are definitely a tease. And, sometimes, they are ultra-violent. The intention was not to be offensive or crass, yet the plays do not skimp on shocks. There are no kitchen sinks here. These are the stories of strong, smart women fighting almost supernatural elements — forces of evil as persistent and unpredictable as a raging storm or a fatal diagnosis. And the men don't get off any lighter, do they?

These plays are presented in this limited edition to coincide with various productions in Chicago. If you've attended any of these performances, we thank you for your interest in reading this text. If you missed these shows and are reading these plays after the curtain falls, we invite you to share *Beautiful Women in Terrible Trouble* with other patrons, actors, directors, producers, or anyone else who wants theatre to be different or be — dare we say? — SHOCKING.

* * *

WITNESS TO AN ACCIDENT

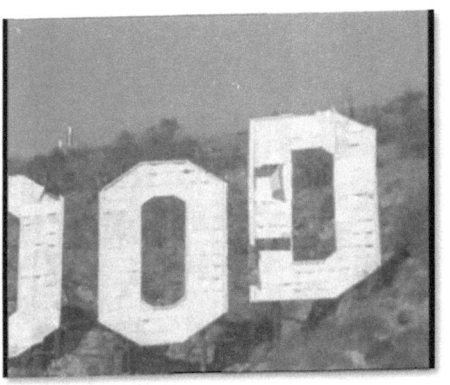

CAST OF CHARACTERS (in order of appearance)

    LILLIAN, a young woman

    NURSE KISSUM, a young woman

    DR. FREDERICKS, a woman

    AGATHA MOLL, a young woman

    RAY PENDARSKY, an older man

    DEAN FOSTER, an older man

    THE ORDERLY, a young man

    NANCY 1, a girl

    NANCY 2, a girl

    Plus a number of females to portray DINNER
    GUESTS, PATIENTS, A FILM CREW, and FIGURES

THE SETTING

    Hollywood, California in the late 1950s

THE SCENE

    "The Hotel" (a hospital), also: a film
    executive's office, a studio lot, an apartment
    (without furniture), a doctor's office, a
    corridor, and various implied rooms.

    Exits stage left and stage right.

ACT I

SCENE 1

LILLIAN, <u>in a yellow dress</u>, sits
at a simple table, surrounded by
female DINNER GUESTS, all wearing
<u>white gowns</u>.

Outside, there is a rainstorm,
distant.

As LILLIAN speaks, she mimes
eating and drinking.

                LILLIAN
I said, Mr. Bogart, Mr. Bogart, I know that you like
your *sailing* and your *scotch* and *acting*, but to
imagine that you *like* me as well! I can't believe it.
He's watched me grow up. I would draw pictures of him
wearing funny hats and slip them under his door of his
guest bungalow. He never said a word about them.
Perhaps the drawings got picked up and thrown out by a
thoughtless maid. But as I got older, my drawings
were getting more and more ribald. He'd come to visit
us about twice a year at that point, to drink with my
father and talk about the movie business. I could
hear them through my own bedroom door, late into the
night, over aromatic cigars and strong drinks. I'd
press my ear to the door and hear Bogie's soft rumble
of a voice, like distant thunder to my father's
quicker lightning, as they made plans for vacations
where everyone, including me, was invited, and he'd
take us *sailing*, and teach me, little Lillian, what
was required in a beautiful and soft first mate.

                Enter NURSE KISSUM, in white,
                interrupting.

                NURSE
Lillian...

                The DINNER GUESTS break off,
                moving to distant corners, each

          with their own ticks and
          affectations. <u>These are not
          guests at a party</u>, but PATIENTS in
          a sanitarium.

          NURSE (Continued)
Enough stories. Why don't you take a nap? It's
raining.

          LILLIAN nods.

          The NURSE passes to exit.

          One by one, the PATIENTS gather
          back where they began, LILLIAN a
          magnet. When they are all seated
          again...

          LILLIAN
So it's spring, perfect sailing weather, and—

          Enter DR. FREDERICKS, in white.

          With her is another young woman,
          who wears cocktail dress and a
          large, fashionable hat.

          This is AGATHA MOLL.

          DR. FREDERICKS
Hello, everyone. We have a new guest at The Hotel.
Her name is Agatha. She'll be in Room 11. Please
make her comfortable. Agatha, these are our other
guests. Introduce yourselves. Lillian: I want you to
be nice.

          DR. FREDERICKS exits.

          Agatha enters the fold, taking a
          few great, confident steps.

AGATHA

Would one of you tell me where the ladies' powder room
is located?

LILLIAN

Down that corridor.

AGATHA

Thank you.

AGATHA exits.

LILLIAN

I don't suppose any of you recognized her? You've
been in here so long you've not kept up with the
papers. But. That... is Agatha Moll - star of *Beach
Fun*, out just recently, with Rodney Rubisio, who
changed his name to Rod Robinson. Also known as: Rod
the Bod. And still I see no recognition in your
faces. Do you even know who Humphrey Bogart is?

AGATHA returns.

AGATHA
(Gesturing back)
There are no mirrors.

LILLIAN

But of course. We don't want a breakage. Glass can
be dangerous. Your face is perfection, dear. Come
here. Have the chair beside me.

AGATHA hesitates then sits.

LILLIAN (Continued)

I like your hat.

AGATHA slowly removes the hat.

3

AGATHA
I forgot that I was wearing it.

LILLIAN
You're very fancy today.

AGATHA
Yes. I know. I was to meet someone special. And I thought this was appropriate. But, now that I look at myself, it is a bit much.

LILLIAN
Don't feel self-conscience, my dear. The dress and hat fit your polished shine. You've studied elocution. And manners. Can you balance a book on your head? Your back is so straight. Former model is my guess. Before other adventures. Twirling in hemmed dresses outside ladies' boutiques at Hollywood and Highland. Spotted by someone? Someone important? Someone who thinks they can help you. And they *do*. Has a conversation with your mother about a job in the secretarial pool. Or perhaps wants to speak with your father, but can't because he's gone off to Texas the year before in the hopes of striking oil. The man gets you a job at the studio, a personal assistant to a charming executive... Am I getting warm?

AGATHA
You know me.

LILLIAN
I do. I'm Lillian.

AGATHA
Have you not been here long?

LILLIAN
Actually, I have. I have a friend who sneaks me magazines. I dabble in the Hollywood editions.

AGATHA
You must like it here, since you stay.

LILLIAN
They call it The Hotel. But hotels let you check out.

AGATHA

I'm going to leave. Don't worry about that. This is just for a few days.

> Pause. LILLIAN dismisses the others. When they're gone from earshot, she continues.

LILLIAN

What put you here? You can tell me. I'm an actress, too, you see? Actually, we're all ladies of stage and screen at The Hotel. It's the specialty of this place. And you can share all about yourself with me. I'm discreet. Discretion is not normally part of an actor's trade, but in this case—

AGATHA

What were you in?

LILLIAN

Great debt. It's hard to survive in this town when you're not Agatha Moll.

AGATHA

Your estimation is exaggerated. I've only done one picture.

LILLIAN

One that did very well, if I believe the publicist gossip that made it into the trades. May I ask you a question? I'm pretty, yes? Prettier than you? Well that wasn't enough. And don't tell me you can act. You've had no training. Those not trained cannot act.

AGATHA

I never wanted to be an actress. I was sort of... forced. But I wasn't terr—

LILLIAN

I can't get in the door by forcing a shoulder and they've opened it for you with smiles on their faces. Life is like that. Some people just have it handed to
(MORE)

                        LILLIAN (Continued)
them when they know nothing. Those in power have
special detection abilities; they can put to the curb
anyone, with nothing more than a subjective dismissal,
when they know nothing, *nothing*, of what is true. In
this town, no one knows anything. Keep that in your
head, if there's room.
            (Pause)
You haven't answered my question.

                        AGATHA
You are pretty.

                        LILLIAN
Another: are you insane?

                        AGATHA
Ins—

                        LILLIAN
Because you are *here*. And you wouldn't be here if you
weren't a cuckoo. Am I right?

                        AGATHA
As far as I know, my head is on straight. I am the
most reasonable and rationale person I know. Is
everyone here a, a cuckoo?

                        LILLIAN
Yes. Cuckoo. But I don't want to prejudice the new
girl on the degrees. You'll have to detect that in
your own conversations with the ladies. But. Agatha
Moll. If you are not... troubled... are you a spy?
Or a reporter? Or doing something as cheap as
studying us to portray a far cry version of us in a
palpable way to a very general public?

                        AGATHA
I'm not here for a character. But. Okay. I hear
your question. Why am I here? You're sizing me up.
Wondering about my own degree of cuckoo.

                        LILLIAN
I size up everyone. You're doing it to me, too, I
think.
            (MORE)

6

LILLIAN (Continued)
(Gesturing)
Which of these girls is the most unhinged? Which
might just bore me with babble; which might try to
strangle me with a bedsheet? Take a guess. You're
looking for the ones that drool, or the ones that
masturbate? It's harder to detect than you might
think. It takes years of practice.

AGATHA
So which one are you? A strangler?

LILLIAN
(Laughs)
But of course! Of *course*. Of course.
(She reaches out her hands then pulls back)

AGATHA
I like to stand on shoulders. You're the giant here.
You tell *me* who is whom.

LILLIAN
But my guesses are all wrong! You'll learn about
things in your own time. What's fun in life if not
discovery? Eh hem. So. Why are you here? Are.
You. A. Spy?

AGATHA
What do I get for spilling beans? If I give you
stories of how I made scenes in restaurants, there
must be some reward. Tit-for-tat.

LILLIAN
You will have an interesting time here. Film lots
don't usually teach pretty girls street smarts.
You're already trading sexual favors for cigarettes.
I have met my match. Maybe we should switch places
for a day and see if anyone notices. Okay, Ms. Agatha
Moll. If you tell me. If... you tell me *why* you have
checked into this place...I will give you something in
return. A treasure. Beyond your wildest. It's a
clue. This clue leads to the great secret of The
Hotel. The great, dark, very, very important, very
secret secret that only *I* know...

                    AGATHA
Well. Lillian, is it? That *is* a temptation. I will
take your clue. And raise you one of mine. Who goes
first?

                    LILLIAN
You. Tit-for-tat.

                    AGATHA
I never trust a stranger.

                    LILLIAN
Well in this case... you kinda have to...

                    AGATHA
I am not insane. I am in this place for one reason:
to keep me from talking to anyone in this town.
Including you. I know something that no one else
knows... And instead of going to meet someone special,
I find myself here. Where I will, for a time, stay
quiet.
          (Pause)
I'll let you chew on that a few days.
          (Pause)
Do you understand? How was my elocution?

                    LILLIAN
I wonder, little starling, if you've studied
elocution... or electrocution. Because I can see the
future. I can predict who will be applied certain
therapies. Shock, for example. And, I think... it
will be you... who will be shocked.

                    AGATHA
I can take it. I'm used to shock.

                    LILLIAN
We'll see.

                    AGATHA
So what it is you're going to tell me in return for
the tip of my iceberg?

                         LILLIAN
All right. Yes. Here.
              (Long Pause)
Find. The. Witness. And you shall be free.

                    Lights fade.

ACT I

SCENE 2

The office of RAY PENDARSKY.

Ray leans back in his chair. A telephone receiver is balanced on his shoulder. He puffs an unlit cigar.

At last, someone rejoins him on the phone line...

                    RAY
          (Into phone)
Yes, I'm still here. Yes, I know. I understand. I realize it's important. This is my number one priority. Yes. I've been meaning to. Yes. Is that so?

                    AGATHA enters carrying a pad and a
                    pencil.

                    RAY motions her down into the
                    chair across from his desk.

                    RAY (Continued)
Uh huh. Okay. Yes. Thank you for the call. I'll consider it. Let me phone you... day after tomorrow. Yes, I've got a lot of important meetings. Not a problem? Good. I'll be in touch. Goodbye.
          (Hangs up, unconcerned)
That was the damn hospital.

                    AGATHA
Oh. How is she doing?

                    RAY
Worse. They want me to come down.

                    AGATHA
What did she do now?

10

RAY

You don't want to know.

AGATHA

I'm sorry, Mr. Pendarsky.

RAY

Forget it. You're too young to be bothered with my
family trouble. One day she's your little girl, in
knee socks and drawing pictures at the kitchen table;
you never think the girl's gonna have a bad day in her
life, with all she has - between me and her mother,
the ex-. And then a couple years pass and you go a
place you never knew existed. People change.
Opportunities come and others pass you by. Divorce.
We all change in time. But to...
        (Snaps fingers)
Snap. Overnight. You just don't want to see your
little baby suffer. But like I said... you're too
young to be burdened by my family trouble.
        (Pause)
Say, doll. With Shirley, you know, in her condition,
I am at a tipping point... There's a decision I've
needed to make for some time, and it's time to shit or
get off the pot. I need a new body for that beach
picture. Was at the casting office all day yesterday
looking at kids under contract, few who weren't, and I
really didn't see any with promise. Wasted the whole
day arguing with that goddamn *Foster*. Good director,
but a pain in the ass! I'm glad you weren't here when
I got back. I was in a mood. But then last night.
Drinking a whiskey at my place and looking out at the
twinkling lights of the Hollywood Hills, I thought of
a solution...

AGATHA

Oh, no—

RAY

You wanna be in pictures?

AGATHA

I've never acted. Not even the high school play.
Only just the modeling.

RAY

Can you sing?

11

                    AGATHA
Not really.

                    RAY
Dance?

          She shakes her head.

                    RAY (Continued)
I still believe the picture needs an unknown face. On
that one point alone, Foster and I agree.

                    AGATHA
I hear Dean Foster can be difficult.

                    RAY
He's an ass. But Shirley liked him. Foster's got a
reputation for decent comedies, so I feel, in that
regard, at least, we've got some credibility for the
poster and with the critics. Mostly, see, I'd back a
name actress. I'm usually the one shoveling casting
down my directors' throats. Tellin' them they can't
hire some cigarette girl they met the week before.
But this time, I just don't feel right about it.
That's why I told him to hire my little girl. She
needed a break. She'd been hitting every audition in
town. And she was good. She really wanted to be in
pictures. But now this thing with the hospital. I
can't hold the shoot any longer. Cameras gotta roll
or I'm out six-hundred thousand on a goddamn *beach*
movie!

                    AGATHA
I'm sorry, Mr. Pendarsky. I wish I could help.

                    RAY
Come on! Every girl under twenty-one in this town can
act. Or at least lies and tells me so.

                    AGATHA
I never really thought about it. I like doing this
work.

                    RAY
So you tell me. Every day. You've made your choice.
                    (MORE)

RAY (Continued)

You're always so damn confident, aren't you?
          (Smiles)
I didn't think you'd be this way after these few
months. Thought: give it time. She makes five
hundred pots of coffee and types a thousand memos and
she'll be asking me what I can do for her and how
soon. Because this - this! - is a waste of time and
talent. Being my secretary. No glamour. No glamour
at all. Hell, you work *at a studio*! Haven't you
caught the bug yet? Every secretary I've ever had -
good or bad - has lobbied for scrap in the worst
pictures this studio has ever made or considered
making! This, this, this job is not a job of
integrity. It's a jumping off point. You know this,
Agatha, *you know this*! It's a ladder and you're on
the first rung. The first! You've got to get up
there so we can look at you.

                    AGATHA
I just want to be honest.

                    RAY
More money in lying... Listen...
          (Starts writing)
What do you want, Agatha? What do you want?

                    AGATHA
I'm a very private person. I have parts of myself
that I don't feel comfortable with. I don't think the
public will want to know all that.

                    RAY
Skeletons in your closet? Baby at fourteen? What is
it?

                    AGATHA
Nothing like that, Mr. Pendarsky.

                    RAY
Are you worried about being judged?

                    AGATHA
Yes. But it's more than that. I am Agatha Moll and I
am your secretary. This I know. I know where I live,
          (MORE)

13

AGATHA (Continued)
what kinds of foods I like, everything about Agatha
Moll. I, I like being grounded in a certain reality.
Even when I model, I am Agatha Moll modeling. Acting
is different. I'm not me.

RAY
Didn't you ever play dress up when you were a kid?

AGATHA
Not really.

RAY
You're mother ever make you a princess costume? You
ever have a tea party with your dolls? You ever kiss
Fabian's picture or call yourself Mrs. Presley?

AGATHA
I prefer Harry Belafonte.

RAY
Well, he lives down the street from me, so I will have
to introduce you. Point is this: you have got to,
have to, musta wanted to pretend something, someone,
anything, anyone. It's who we are.

AGATHA
You make a compelling case.

RAY
What you have is a common fear. Common problem. It's
not about identity. It's about judgment. But I have
to ask... if you fear being judged, whether you
recognize it or not, why do modeling? It's nothing
but critical eyes.

AGATHA
My sister told me I should try it.

RAY
Maybe you should ask your sister about this?

AGATHA
I'm a very private person.

Long pause.

RAY finishes what he's writing.
He folds the paper, places it in
an envelope and seals it.

RAY
I'm going to send you to the lot with a memo. Don't
open it. Take it to Dean Foster. Tell him it's from
me and then do whatever he says.

AGATHA
I really don't think I should—

RAY
No, forget the acting. You've convinced me. This is
something else. Just be a good girl and get it done.

She takes the sealed memo.
Slowly, she stands.

AGATHA
I will... get it done.

Lights fade.

ACT I

SCENE 3

A film set. AGATHA enters.

DEAN FOSTER answers quiet
questions from his FILM CREW, a
few women surrounding him.

AGATHA waits patiently for a
signal.

FOSTER spots her out of the corner
of his eye and turns, annoyed.

                    FOSTER
You here for me?

                    AGATHA
I'm from Ray Pendarsky's office.

                    FOSTER
You his secretary?

                    AGATHA
Yes. I have a message.

                    She holds out the memo. He takes
                    it, opens the envelope, and reads.

                    FOSTER
Is he kidding?

                    AGATHA
I'm sorry, I—

                    FOSTER
I said, is he kidding?

                    AGATHA
          (Nervous)
I'm sorry. I don't know what the note—

16

                    FOSTER
Is he trying to get me thrown in jail?

                    AGATHA
Jail?

                    FOSTER
How old are you, kid? Seventeen?

                    AGATHA
Ninetee—

                    FOSTER
'Cos I'm not going back to jail for that.

                    He winks at the crew, paces.

                    AGATHA doesn't know what to do.

                    AGATHA
I'm sorry. He didn't tell me what it said in the
memo.

                    FOSTER
          (To FILM CREW)
Out. Out. Everyone out. Clear the set, please.
Thank you. Goodbye.

                    FOSTER rushes everyone offstage
                    until he is left with only AGATHA.

                    FOSTER (Continued)
Remove your shoes.

                    AGATHA
What?

                    FOSTER
Lose the heels.
          (No compliance)
Ray said you had to do whatever I said. He wrote it
down. Said he'd fire you.

                    AGATHA
Fire me?

                    FOSTER
I'm not making this up, sister. You have to do it.

                    Long pause.

                    AGATHA
Take off my shoes?

                    FOSTER
Simple request.

                    She slowly takes off both of her
                    high-heeled shoes.

                    FOSTER
The hose.

                    AGATHA
My pantyhose?

                    FOSTER
Come on, dummy. Off.

                    AGATHA
I don't know if—

                    FOSTER
You want to keep your job, don't ya? I hear Ray pays
pretty well. Better than the local grocery store.

                    She debates, nervous.

                    At last, she rolls her eyes, with
                    a look of "get it over with" and
                    discreetly slips down her
                    pantyhose.

          FOSTER comes forward. He gets on
          his knees in front of her and
          stares at her bare legs.

          FOSTER (Continued)

On your toes.

          AGATHA

Can I get a 'please' this time?

          FOSTER

No.

          She holds.

          FOSTER (Continued)

Fine. Please!

          Like a ballerina, she rises onto
          her toes.

          FOSTER continues to stare at her
          legs. He reaches out like he
          might just caress her calves, but
          abruptly stands up.

          FOSTER (Continued)

Okay.

          She comes down off her toes. He
          turns his back on her, thinking.

          Quickly, he turns and gives her
          the memo.

          FOSTER (Continued)

Oh, what I wouldn't do to be a fat executive in this
town. Know nothing about making a picture. But know
what makes me tick.
        (Pause)
You smell good. What's that perfume?

AGATHA

Diorissimo.
          (Reads memo then folds it)
Oh. I see.

FOSTER

What matters most in this beach picture are the legs
of the love interest. They're mentioned about fifteen
times in the script and it's the reason the boy
notices her on the beach. We can make giant bugs
attack the capitol, but we can't make a girl with
perfect gams. We have to *find* her.

AGATHA

And how are mine?

FOSTER

Nice. You must have been a model.

AGATHA

I was.

FOSTER

Everyone in this town was a model at some point. I
don't suppose you can act?

AGATHA

I've never done it before.

FOSTER

Hmmm.
          (Pause, warming)
Listen, I'm sorry about... barking at you. These
fucking executives! Ahhh! I had three girls
yesterday I thought were great, but the big guy
wouldn't bless 'em. It was a volcanic day. Look, all
I want to do is get this picture finished so I can
move on to the next. It's an assembly line, see. And
I had the whole thing moving and, and - WHAM! - a big
ol' kink. I roll with punches, but can't roll without
a girl.
          (Pause)
Get back to that chicken coop you work in. Tell him
I'll think about it.

AGATHA

I'm not an actress.

FOSTER

I know. You're a secretary.

AGATHA

I mean, not even on the side. I've never acted. Only the modeling.

FOSTER

Who gives a shit about acting in this town? Certainly not Ray Pendarsky.

AGATHA

But—

FOSTER

I'm looking for faces. I'm looking for voices. I'm looking for legs. I don't care if you want to be the next Brando. I don't make those kinds of pictures. You want an Oscar, go charm Elia Kazan.

AGATHA
          (Not convinced)
I see...

FOSTER

What's the matter? Afraid you'll lose your secretarial chops?

AGATHA

No.

FOSTER

Afraid of a fat paycheck?

AGATHA

No.

FOSTER

Then why the cold feet at the end of those hot legs?

AGATHA

I'm afraid of losing myself.

FOSTER

Does that have to do with being judged? Because Ray
says -- in the memo -- says go easy on you and don't
be a judge.

AGATHA

But you did do just that.

FOSTER

Well. I don't have a habit of completely listening to
the brass, if you know what I mean. So, basically...
I'm not afraid of anything. But you are.

AGATHA

I'm afraid of lots of things. Like becoming someone
I'm not.

FOSTER

Don't worry. Fame changes nothing but who pays for
lunch.
                    (Pause)
Maybe I still don't understand. Look, just tell
Pendarsky I'll think about it. Nothing's set in
stone. It's not like you've signed a contract.

AGATHA

Okay.

FOSTER

Let's get you a script. Do a test. There're some
steps ahead, so you've got plenty of time to break my
heart.

                    AGATHA, at last, smiles then
                    exits.

                    FOSTER (Continued)
          (To himself)
Diorissimo.
          (Calling)
Where the hell is everyone!

                    Lights fade.

ACT I

SCENE 4

Dim lights rise.

NURSE KISSAM walks past a series
of doors — the rooms of patients,
peering in and checking off a list
on her clipboard.

Enter THE ORDERLY — a young man
dressed in white clothes with an
outwardly friendly, but somehow
strange smile on his face.

The NURSE startles and appears a
little frightened.

                    THE ORDERLY
Don' be scared. It's me.

                    NURSE
I'm not scared.

                    THE ORDERLY comes forward and
                    peers in a small window cut in the
                    door.

                    THE ORDERLY
New arrival?

                    NURSE
Just before supper. During the storm.

                    THE ORDERLY
What if I wake her up?

                    NURSE
When are you going to see her?

                    THE ORDERLY
Why? You the mother hen?

                    NURSE
Just curious.

                    She starts to move past him.

                    THE ORDERLY
You in a hurry?

                    NURSE
Dr. Fredericks wanted to see me when I was finished.

                    THE ORDERLY
She doesn't want to see you.

                    NURSE
She said that she—

                    THE ORDERLY
She didn't say nothin'. So... why you in such a
hurry?

                    NURSE
I... I don't know what you want me to say.

                    THE ORDERLY
Just... say what you always say. Say it.

                    He suddenly grabs her around the
                    waist and pulls her in.

                    THE ORDERLY (Continued)
          (Soft and severe)
Say it.

                    The NURSE leans forward to his ear
                    and whispers something unheard.

                    THE ORDERLY (Continued)
I love it when you say that.

THE ORDERLY waves a hand in front
of her face, then smiles, lets her
out of his arms, and exits,
slapping the NURSE on the behind
as he moves past to offstage.

The NURSE continues down the dark
corridor. She slows when she
hears...

SOUND: Soft music coming from one
of the rooms. It's a retro
bubblegum pop song.

She puts her ear to the door and
listens. After a moment, she
moves along, exiting.

Pause.

THE ORDERLY enters again. He,
too, hears the music. He comes to
the door, smiles, frowns, smiles
again, and then knocks.

ACT I

SCENE 5

AGATHA sits on her bed in The
Hotel listening to a pop song on a
small, portable radio. There is a
knock at the door. She sits up.
She wears only her undergarments.

                    AGATHA
Just a moment...

                    AGATHA sees her cocktail dress
                    over a chair and begins to slip it
                    back on.

                    While she is doing so, the door
                    slowly opens to reveal THE
                    ORDERLY.

                    AGATHA (Continued)
I asked you to wait.

                    THE ORDERLY
This ain't your door, lady. This is my door.

                    AGATHA
This is my room.

                    THE ORDERLY
I've been in this room a thousand times. You been in
it one night.

                    THE ORDERLY enters and slowly
                    inspects the room. He sees the
                    source of the music: a radio sits
                    on the night table. He walks to it
                    and switches it off.

                    THE ORDERLY (Continued)
No radios.

                    AGATHA
I found it under the bed. When I stored my bag.

                    THE ORDERLY
Then it was smuggled.

                              He unplugs the radio from the wall
                              and, business-like, wraps the
                              radio in its chord and sets it on
                              the bed. Then, going to the
                              closet, he takes down a gown from
                              a hanger.

                    THE ORDERLY (Continued)
You have to lose your fancy dress.

                              He tosses the gown at her and she
                              catches it.

                    THE ORDERLY (Continued)
Gown's the rules after first day. Go ahead. Can't
keep wearing that bit of black. Start to smell.
Diorissimo can't cover that forever.

                    AGATHA
I'll... change in a minute.

                    THE ORDERLY
You'll do it now.

                    AGATHA
Who *are* you?

                    THE ORDERLY
I'm the orderly. I keep things ordered. Orders say
you wear a gown.

                              AGATHA looks down at her dress,
                              then the gown.

THE ORDERLY (Continued)
Look, we got off on the wrong foot. Rules, rules,
rules. Place runs on rules. Everyone wears the angel
white. Hotel feels like heaven. Girls in white, all
Cherubic. Pretty girl like you can pull off a potato
sack so don't feel shy about losing your party hat.
        (No response)
Tell you a secret. I love the white myself. Never
looked better, never felt better, than when I'm in the
white. Wear it well, don't you think? Check out the
buttons. Oops, missed one. There. I'd pass an
inspection.
        (Pause, then gesturing)
You gonna wear it, or do I have to get physical?

                AGATHA
I want to see the nurse.

                THE ORDERLY
You think she'd reverse my decision? No appeals here.
This ain't a court of law. Gotta wear a gown, new
girl. Now chop-chop. Schedule to keep. It's past
lights out.

                AGATHA
Fine. Would you please step outside while I-?

                THE ORDERLY
No. We've reached an impasse. You know what that is,
don'tcha?

                AGATHA
Yes.

                THE ORDERLY
We're at a point of distrust in our relationship. I
walk out, get distracted, don't come back for ten or
fifteen, and then I see you still lounging in your
puffy skirt. Maybe put back on your fancy hat.
Everyone here wears a gown.

                AGATHA
Why?

THE ORDERLY
A questioner. Great. Love those.

AGATHA
You're to work on my head, not my body.

THE ORDERLY
Not your body? Hmmm. Gowns provide a consistency to
the proceedings. Uniform. Like you're becoming a
soldier in the U.S. Army. One size fits all.

AGATHA
Am I an angel or a soldier?

THE ORDERLY
Is there a difference? And don't get smart with me.
If you think this makes it better, consider you're
like a newborn babe in swaddling clothes. Strip away
the past.
          (Moves forward)
Plus... *new girl*... I happen to think gowns is sexier
than skirts. You put it on. Show you I'm right. I
wish gowns were S.O.P. throughout this fair state of
California. Hell, throughout the whole country, sea
to shiny sea. Gowns is beautiful.

AGATHA
What's your name?

THE ORDERLY
I'm the orderly. Like I said. Just call me that.
And stop dragging your pretty toes.

                         He stares at her. She doesn't
                         move. He steps into her and pins
                         her to the wall. He roughly pulls
                         down the shoulder of her dress.

AGATHA
You'll rip it!

THE ORDERLY
I will. I'll rip off the whole goddamn thing! Or you
can slip it off and hand it to me and I'll put it in a
                    (MORE)

                        THE ORDERLY (Continued)
box for you. It won't be touched the whole time
you're here. Not by anybody.
            (Pause)
This isn't a point of debate, this gown! It's the
rule!

                              He backs up, like he might take a
                              swing at her.

                              She straightens. Almost daringly,
                              she strips out of her dress and
                              puts the gown on over her head.

                              When she's finished, he steps
                              forward and pins her once more to
                              the wall. He reaches up under her
                              gown, fondling her.

                        THE ORDERLY (Continued)
            (Breathless)
See? I told you gowns were sexier than skirts.

                              She screams and he covers her
                              mouth.

                              He continues touching her to the
                              point of audience discomfort then
                              suddenly breaks away.

                              He picks up the radio from the bed
                              and exits, firmly closing the door
                              behind.

                              Blackout.

ACT I

SCENE 6

An apartment without furniture.

DEAN FOSTER reclines on the floor,
shirtless. He's smoking and stubs
it out.

After a moment, AGATHA enters
wearing a man's robe.

FOSTER

Am I dreaming?

AGATHA

What do you mean?

FOSTER

I mean: here you are.

AGATHA

You're not dreaming. It's me.

AGATHA comes closer then crawls
into him, snuggling.

AGATHA (Continued)

I meant to ask. But you distracted me. Where's all
your furniture?

FOSTER

Sold it in a moment of panic.

AGATHA

Panic?

FOSTER

That I was no longer fashionable.

AGATHA

You don't seem to be the type to panic about fashion.

FOSTER

I live in L.A. Of course I panic about things
fashionable. It may not always be clothes, though, or
furniture. Just don't want to become obsolete.

AGATHA

You'll never be obsolete, Herr Director.

She kisses him.

FOSTER

Are you sure this isn't a dream?

She kisses him again, longer.

AGATHA

It *is* a dream. None of this is real. You've had a
dream that after a hard day of shooting me in water,
you've let your fantasies get the best of you. You
asked me out for dinner to discuss my performance.
You given me too much table wine and told me funny
stories about people I don't know — some of them
seated only a few tables from us at the restaurant.
And then, before you wake up, you decided to kiss me,
just to see how things might play out. I let you do
it, because I've realized suddenly that you're not the
bull you've been all day, shouting at cameramen and
boys and girls in beachwear to do this, do that, stand
here, do it better, or you're fired—!

FOSTER

I didn't threaten anyone.

AGATHA

Not today.

FOSTER

Do I do that a lot?
          (Reads her face)
Shit. I hope no one takes me seriously.

AGATHA

You fired me once.

32

FOSTER
I did?

AGATHA
The second day of shooting. Because I couldn't hula
hoop. You said, "That hoop better stay right at your
hips at least once today or don't bother showing up
for makeup tomorrow."

FOSTER
Ah... That was not a part of my dream. This is. So
what happened next?

AGATHA
So after dinner, you walked me back towards your
private car, holding my hand. And then you paid the
driver fifty dollars to go home and you drove me down
Sunset to this room, which you say you own, but seems
strangely like where a transient squats for a night.
And you kissed me up the stairs, onto the floor, and
here. Then you told me to wash up. And it's in the
bathroom that I find any evidence of domesticity.
This robe. Your tooth-brush. Coconut shampoo. A
razor.

FOSTER
You forgot the full ashtray.

AGATHA
Do you take many girls here?

FOSTER
Take them? You make it sound predatory.

AGATHA
You know what I mean. But... I suppose... if this
apartment is a love nest, you'd need at least a
mattress.

FOSTER
Which is more revealing: an empty room with a single
mattress, or just an empty room?

AGATHA
Is it true about your un-fashionable furniture?

                    FOSTER
What's true is that you are beautiful.

                    AGATHA
Don't change the subject.

                    FOSTER
That's the only subject I want to discuss. You
haven't been to the rushes.

                    AGATHA
You haven't invited me.

                    FOSTER
You are going to be a star.

                    AGATHA's face changes. She sits
                    up, rubs his chest.

                    AGATHA
A star.

                    FOSTER
Yes. Don't you want that?

                    AGATHA
Why do actors like death scenes?

                    FOSTER
Pardon?

                    AGATHA
Death scenes.

                    FOSTER
Do you want a death scene? You've seen the latest
pages. No one goes out like Scarface in a teen
picture. Unless you count West Side Story. But this
isn't that.

                    AGATHA
If you're an actor, you will probably die.

FOSTER

I got news for you, kid. Everybody dies. Think of
it: as an actor, you get the chance to get adjusted to
dying more than the average person. You think about
drowning. What it would be like, how to "act" that.
You figure it all out before film rolls. You've
thought of how the face will look bloated in sea-salt,
you think about running out of breath. Maybe you hold
your breath for two minutes to get some pain in your
lungs.

AGATHA

You think we must all really prepare like that—

FOSTER

You consider how your character would react to
drowning... Surprise? Inevitability? Shock?

AGATHA

There's a difference between shock and surprise?

FOSTER

Sure there is. Show me surprise.

AGATHA makes a face.

FOSTER (Continued)

Now show me shock.

AGATHA does the face.

FOSTER (Continued)

That's the same.

AGATHA

That's what I'm saying.

FOSTER

Here's a motivation. Just now, I got you pregnant.

AGATHA

Am I doing surprise or shock?

FOSTER

All right. I suppose you would know if it was a surprise based on your time of the month. It would have to be shock. Let me choose another one. Okay here. You have just won a million dollars.

AGATHA does a face.

FOSTER (Continued)

Perfect surprise. Now you've just heard that your sister is dead.

AGATHA

I *would* be shocked.

FOSTER

Coming to my side, huh?

AGATHA

I'd be shocked because she's already dead.

FOSTER

Shit.

AGATHA

She died when I was sixteen. In a car crash.

FOSTER

Oh. I'm sorry. I feel like a jerk.

AGATHA

I don't remember much of how I felt in that moment when I heard the news. Probably a mix of both surprise and shock. Shocked that she was gone so suddenly; surprised that it wasn't me, too, as I was supposed to be in the car. I had a sudden call for a modeling job at a department store. So she dropped me off at the spot and went on into the Valley and... rolled six times.

                        FOSTER
Fate. Modeling saved your life. Of course. You're
beautiful. Like I said.
            (Pause)
You're manifesting neither surprise nor shock on your
face when I compliment you. So you must know that that
part is a little bit true.

                        AGATHA
All that matters is that you think so.

                        FOSTER
I'm sorry about your sister.

                Pause.

                        AGATHA
            (Changing subject)
Tell me more about shock.

                        FOSTER
Shock. Shock. You like shock. Okay. Let me show
you something very, very shocking...

                        He rolls over on her and begins
                        kissing her passionately on the
                        floor.

                        Lights fade.

ACT I

SCENE 7

The Hotel.

AGATHA lays on her bed in
darkness. She cries softly.
She's having a bad dream. She
twists in the sheets, protesting
something unseen.

At last, she springs up –
SCREAMING!

Lights blast in the corner of the
room, revealing two women wearing
plain, featureless masks over
their faces.

This is NANCY 1 and NANCY 2. They
look very similar, but are not
identical.

AGATHA notices the two and jumps.

                    NANCY 1 | NANCY 2
Is that shock?

                    AGATHA pulls the sheets up,
                    petrified.

                    NANCY 1 | NANCY 2
Don't you recognize me?

                    AGATHA
Yes... But you're dead. Nancy.

                    NANCY 2
I wanted to pay you a visit, but the front desk has
such strict policies about guests.

                    NANCY 1
Who was that man? The one in white. He was cute.

                    AGATHA
He's ugly. And you're a dream.

                    NANCY 1
I'm real. Just ask her.

                    NANCY 2
She's real. I vouch for her.

                    AGATHA
My sister Nancy died four years ago.

                    NANCY 1
I didn't die, kiddo. I just split in two.

                    NANCY 2
Re-grown parts. Arms. Legs. Boobs. Everything.

                    AGATHA
This is a nightmare. I'm in a strange place. When
that happens, I dream weird dreams. I want you to go
away now.

                    NANCY 1
I'm here to help you, Agatha. So you shouldn't be
scared of me. I came to tell you a secret.

                    NANCY 2
Yes. That Lillian is just outside the door. She's
listening to this conversation. She can only hear
half of it. *Your* half.

                    NANCY 1
So you should keep you voice very, very low.

                    AGATHA rises and steps to the
                    door.

                    NANCY 2
Don't open it. We're going to play a little trick on
her. I want you to repeat after me, so she hears what
we want her to hear.

NANCY 1
Say: I know how you got your yellow dress.

AGATHA
I know how you got your yellow dress.

NANCY 2
Louder.

AGATHA
I-I know how you got your yellow dress.

NANCY 1 and NANCY 2 look at each
other, smile.

NANCY 1
Tell her: I know the name of the witness.

AGATHA
I know the name... the name of the witness.

NANCY 2
The Orderly knows my secret. But he won't tell you.

AGATHA
The Orderly knows my secret. But he won't tell you.

NANCY 1
Get back to your fucking room, bitch.

AGATHA
Y—you should go back to your room.

Pause.

On the other side of the door,
there is movement in the corridor,
the light under the door shifts.
A shadow, leaving.

Pause.

                    AGATHA
How did you know? How did you know she was out there?

                    NANCY 1
We know quite a bit about this place.

                NANCY 1 | NANCY 2
It brought us here.

                    AGATHA
The hospital brought you here.

                    NANCY 2
The Hotel. This place is like no other place on the
earth.

                    NANCY 1
And this place keeps secrets tighter than any twelve
year old girl's diary.

            The two NANCYs laugh.

                    AGATHA
You... you said... something about a witness.

                    NANCY 1
Yes. It doesn't matter if the things you said aren't
true; just that you said them, and that Lillian thinks
they're true.

                    NANCY 2
She's very threatened by you. I suppose she's a
lesbian.

                    AGATHA
You used to think every woman was a lesbian. I
remember that about you. You... judged women very
harshly. You never liked girls... women. You liked
our father, but not our mother. There are certain
girls, I'm told, that prefer the company of boys.

                    NANCY 1
And you are not one of them. Are you?

AGATHA

Dean. I liked his company. But I'm not like you
were. Men wanted you. Boys *and* men... desired you.
They like me, but not with the same desire. If a boy
showed interest, you would cut females from your life
by the dozens until it was just you and him. You had
no use for them. You weren't safe around women.
Women were out to get you, to compete with you. You
told me this over and over.

NANCY 2

I thought you said I was just a weird dream.

AGATHA

I. I know what I said. You just look so real. I
want to touch you. Can I touch you?

AGATHA reaches out her hand—

NANCY 1 | NANCY 2

Are you perhaps confused?

—and then retracts.

AGATHA

Not me. I'm not confused about anything.

NANCY 2

Are you in love?

AGATHA

Who could love that monster?

NANCY 1

The boy in white.

NANCY 2

Are you going to report him?

AGATHA

He didn't do anything that hasn't been done before.

                    NANCY 2
Do you love him?

                    AGATHA
Don't talk like that.

                    NANCY 1
We're not talking about the orderly, silly.
     (Pause)
Do you—

                    NANCY 2
-love him.

                    AGATHA
I can't love someone that's dead.

                    NANCY 1
Who says Dean Foster is dead?

                    AGATHA
The papers.

                    NANCY 2
Sources say otherwise.

                    AGATHA
What? What is that? Dean's— Tell me what you know!
Tell me what you know!

                         A sudden loud screeching and she
                         covers her ears.

                         Blackout.

                         On rise, NANCY 1 and NANCY 2 have
                         vanished.

                         Lights fade.

ACT I

SCENE 8

RAY PENDARSKY is in his office,
shuffling through papers and
gathering his things, as if he is
anxious to find something.

There is a knock at his door.

                    RAY
Who is it?

                    THE ORDERLY
          (Through door)
I'm sorry to bother you, Mr. Pendarsky. It's
important that I speak with you.

                    RAY
Please make an appointment with my secretary for
another day. I'm very busy.

                    THE ORDERLY
          (Through door)
Sorry to burst your bubble, sir. But there's no one
out here. And it's kinda urgent that I speak with
you.

                    RAY
Not today. Not today.

                    RAY continues his searching.

                    THE ORDERLY
          (Through door)
Looking for your last will and testament?

                    RAY looks up, angry.

THE ORDERLY
(Through door)
I've come from The Hotel.

RAY
(Laughs, huffs)
Which one?

THE ORDERLY
(Through door)
The *only* one, Mr. Pendarsky. Or, I guess I should
say, the only one you care about.

RAY stops cold. He puts away the
stacks he's been searching through
and composes himself.

Slowly, he goes to the door and
opens it.

THE ORDERLY stands there in white
hospital uniform.

RAY
You look familiar. You're from The Hotel? Maybe I've
seen you.

THE ORDERLY
(Sarcastic)
Sure, for all those times you stop by. May I come in?

RAY
Sure, sure.

RAY gestures and THE ORDERLY
enters.

RAY
You have news about Shirley?

THE ORDERLY
She sent me to see you.

                              RAY
Sent you? Are you one of her doctors?

                         THE ORDERLY
Not exactly.

                              RAY
I'm sorry about my secretary. I forgot. I put her on
an errand. You timed this perfectly. How'd you get
on the lot? I don't like having visitors from the
hospital. A lot of people around here with big
mouths. Shirley grew up with a lot of them. Saw her
from a young age... playing ball in the lot. Trying
on makeup with the powder girls. Saw some of her
behavior, too. I've made excuses. A few think she's
with her mother in Santa Clarita. If you had to
register at the desk, I hope you showed discretion.

                         THE ORDERLY
Don't worry 'bout it, sir. I'm good with secrets.
And getting in places without being noticed. Not a
soul knows I'm here.

                              RAY
Good. Thank you.

                         THE ORDERLY
Wait. I should amend that.
          (Dreaded pause)
Not a soul but Shirley.

                              RAY
What about Dr. Fredericks?

                         THE ORDERLY
Just Shirley.

                              RAY
Oh. She, she sent you? Are you treating her?

                         THE ORDERLY
I'm kind of a... mentor, I guess you could say.

                              RAY
God, I hope for your sake you're not more than a
mentor. I... I think you better get to the heart of
it.

                    THE ORDERLY
May I sit?

                    RAY
Sure. Here. Take this chair.

                    THE ORDERLY
Say - I don't mean to impose. But do you think.
Well, this is just for a laugh. Do you think it'd be
all right if I sat in *your* chair? My back is killing
me. That's a little wooden chair with a hard back.
You've got the leather. I love leather.

                    RAY
Uh. Be my guest.

                              THE ORDERLY crosses and drops into
                              RAY's chair, letting out a healthy
                              sigh of pleasure, fondling and
                              admiring the leather.

                    THE ORDERLY
Good chair. Good chair!

                    RAY
Thank you.

                    THE ORDERLY
I feel like making a movie!

                    RAY
Well, I suppose that chair does inspire that. A few
producers were in that seat before it came to me.
We've got a lot of pictures completed in my reign, and
the reign of executives that preceded me.

                    THE ORDERLY
Can I tell you about my movie? I've got one that's
surefire.

                    RAY
I don't think it's appropriate—

THE ORDERLY

Starts like this. Close up. Little girl; normal
little girl. Pretty little girl. She has a dream to
be in the movies, like most pretty little girls in
California consider. This girl takes tap dance, takes
all kinds a' lessons. Learns to sing and play the
piano. This can be a montage you understand. I don't
want to bog down the movie with ten years of this
stuff at the beginning. But it's important to
understand her character. She's worked. Real hard.
She's worked her little perfect ass off, pardon my
leer, and now she's ready for the big time. Then, it
is revealed that her father actually *makes* movies.
He's got all the, all the *power*. All the money. He's
got an entire studio. *This* studio. And he could
throw the little girl a bone. Get her a job. Like a
nice daddy should. But when the little girl comes to
him, he says no. He says a bunch of things that make
them both really uncomfortable. And says— Can you
guess where I'm going with this?

RAY

Who are you?

THE ORDERLY

He says he'll get her a starring role. Not because
she's been practicing and she's learned to sing and
learned to tinkle the ivories and learned to actually
be all natural in front of people and play a part.
But he's going to make her a star if she does just
this one... little... thing.

RAY

Did Shirley put you up to this? She's a liar! You
shouldn't trust a thing she says! If you, you
think... this is some sort of, of blackmail, well
you've got another thing coming—

THE ORDERLY

I don't want to blackmail you, Mr. Pendarsky. No. I
came here to tell you that I admire you. I really do.
You're the bee's knees. First, I thought that last
Miss Randy Turner picture was killer. Saw it three
times. I love the bad girls. And she was *bad*. And
second, that whatever games you want to play with your
little girl, I'm really fine with it. I really am!

                        RAY
Get out! Get out of my chair! To insinuate that I—

                        RAY leaps across the desk and
                        grabs THE ORDERLY by his face.

                        RAY (Continued)
            (Cold)
Get out.

                        THE ORDERLY
            (Calmly)
This town's got a side that's lies just beyond the
disappointments. A blackness. Horrors that are like
deep cuts in the skin. People you wouldn't want to
know in a million years.
            (Pause)
I'm one of those people.

                        RAY considers what he's doing and
                        releases THE ORDERLY.

                        RAY
You think I can be intimidated by a poverty wage thug?

                        THE ORDERLY
Yes. You are. You don't know what I'm capable of
doing to Shirley. And, even though you... did what
you did... you still have a' soft spot for your little
girl. Even if you find her a tad... embarrassing.

                        RAY
I thought you were here to protect her. To confront
me. Gallant white knight.

                        THE ORDERLY
No. Actually I'm here to fuck you and then fuck her.

                        RAY punches THE ORDERLY and he
                        falls out of the chair.

                                                    49

                              Slowly, he rises, holding his jaw.

                    THE ORDERLY (Continued)
Interestin'. Been watching too many boxing movies?

                    RAY
What's your name? I'll report you to Dr. Fredericks.
What's your goddamn name?

                    THE ORDERLY
You call the doctor. You do that. Me and the doctor.
We're tight. She's got my back, see? And she owes me
lots of favors. Lots. But it's not my ass that needs
savin'. It's yours.

                    RAY
You can't threaten me.

                    THE ORDERLY
Oh kan-*trare*. Threatening's what I do. But this
isn't about your daughter and the ol' Hotel. This is
about you. This isn't about what you done to her, or
what' you'll do to her when she's out and cured. *If*
she's cured! This is about a certain... beach movie.
It's about boys and girls in the sun. It's about how
things get done in this town. It's about who has the
power. Tomorrow, I want you to fire the director.

                    RAY
Foster's on contract. The picture's nearly through
its shoot.

                    THE ORDERLY
Doesn't matter. I've got friends want him gone.

                    RAY
Did Shirley put you up to this?

                    THE ORDERLY
Shirley don't know nothin'. Yeah, she used to roll in
the sheets with him. But that's not why I'm makin' my
request. You replace Foster and then give him a
message. You tell him. Tell him you know the
witness.

                         RAY
I'm not doing anything. I'm calling the police.

                    THE ORDERLY
Don't do *that*. If one cop shows up at The Hotel, I'll
stick a knife up Shirley's cunt.

                         RAY
I'll have you arrested before you leave the lot.
I'll, I'll drive there and get her out myself tonight.

                    THE ORDERLY
What you have to make this so difficult? You just
have one simple thing to do. Hell, you don't even
like the guy. Look - I'm leaving. You can do what
you want. You make a call and they stop me at the
gate. Just know that if you do, and a part of me
really hopes you do, you will be in so much trouble
you won't be able to shit for a month. You'll be up
to here in the stuff. I'm with interested parties who
don't like it when things don't go there way. Just
release Foster from his contract—

                         RAY
On what grounds?

                    THE ORDERLY
Don't care. Make it up. You release him and give him
my message: you know the witness. And then you're
square. Mum's on Shirl and she stays safe at The
Hotel. Scouts. Honor. But if you don't...

                    THE ORDERLY makes a rising tide of
                    shit gesture, reaching climax at
                    his neck, where he motions a slice
                    of the throat.

                    THE ORDERLY (Continued)
Let's see what you decide...

                    THE ORDERLY exits.

                    Lights fade.

ACT I

SCENE 9

DR. FREDERICKS is seated across from AGATHA in session.

DR. FREDERICKS
There's a test we give. Shall we begin?

AGATHA nods.

DR. FREDERICKS (Continued)
Have you ever talked to yourself in a mirror?

AGATHA
Yes. But—

DR. FREDERICKS
Have you ever been seriously depressed to the point of considering suicide?

AGATHA
Yes. Right after my sister Nancy died.

DR. FREDERICKS
As a child, did you ever feel one or both of your parents did not like you?

AGATHA
Are the questions all this personal?

DR. FREDERICKS
It's the nature of the treatment.

AGATHA
What is the test supposed to indicate?

DR. FREDERICKS
If you're a danger.

AGATHA
To me or to others?

                    DR. FREDERICKS
Do you need me to repeat my last question?

                    AGATHA
No.

                    DR. FREDERICKS
Your answer?

                    AGATHA
My parents loved me.

                    DR. FREDERICKS
Just yes or no.

                    AGATHA
No. I never felt one or both did not like me.

                    DR. FREDERICKS
Did you ever run away from home prior to the age of
fourteen?

                    AGATHA
I packed my bags a few times.

                    DR. FREDERICKS
Did you ever doing something seriously wrong and felt
zero regret?

                    AGATHA
No.

                    DR. FREDERICKS
Has your understanding of what are "normal feelings"
changed over the years?

                    AGATHA
What do you mean?

                    DR. FREDERICKS
Example: your beloved dog is hit by a car. You are
sad for the loss and angry with the driver.

                    AGATHA
Yes, of course.

DR. FREDERICKS
But this happens on the street to a neighbor who is
neither sad nor angry. When you were young, this made
little sense to you, but now that you are older you
understand that it is normal to not show sadness or
anger in certain situations, like grief, but to be
something altogether different.

AGATHA
Death should always make one sad and angry. But I
understand. Walk a mile in someone's shoes. What is
normal? Is that what you're getting at?

DR. FREDERICKS makes a note.

DR. FREDERICKS
Have you ever deliberately caused harm to someone and
then claimed it was an accident?

Long pause.

AGATHA
          (Stalling)
You mean emotional harm?

DR. FREDERICKS
Physical.

AGATHA
How many more questions are there in this test?

DR. FREDERICKS
The test has thirty-six questions.

AGATHA
I don't want to answer any more.

DR. FREDERICKS
We can... pick it up later...
          (Puts down her question sheet)
Did anyone ever tell you about subjective loss? Early
life experience? Depressive reactions?

AGATHA

I've heard those phrases. You've already diagnosed
me, haven't you? I didn't have to finish the test.

DR. FREDERICKS

I'm not *presuming* anything.
(Pause)
One presumes a person remembers how they got to their
destination. What do you remember about arriving
here, at The Hotel?

AGATHA

You mean the feeling of walking in the door?

DR. FREDERICKS

Sure, that, too, if you'd like. But I meant, more
specifically, what do you remember happening to you
just before your check in?

AGATHA

I remember... reading a newspaper. I saw a notice
that, that I can't remember, but... It's all black.
Then I'm driving on the Hollywood Freeway.

DR. FREDERICKS

Which direction?

AGATHA

The Basin. I'm driving fast. But it feels very, very
slow to me. And... And... I've got this address in my
glove box and I think... To be imprisoned for a long
time. I think about escaping and what escape must
feel like. Must feel very strange.

DR. FREDERICKS

You're talking about escape from reality?

AGATHA

I don't know what I'm talking about. You tell me.
Somehow... I thought I would discover something. So
right up until I pulled into the circle outside, I
felt panicked and, and constricted, and then, crossing
into the lobby, a sense of weight coming off my
shoulders.

DR. FREDERICKS

And what about when you registered?

                    AGATHA
I thought... I'll never be found again.

                 DR. FREDERICKS
Did you like this feeling?

                    AGATHA
For about twenty minutes. Now I want to go home. And
then, every moment, like last night, when I wanted to
rush out of this place, I felt that to do so would be
a mistake.

                 DR. FREDERICKS
You're here to get healthy.

                    AGATHA
No. No, not that. That would be very rational,
wouldn't it?

                 DR. FREDERICKS
Then what are you here for?

                    AGATHA
I need to stay here to stay safe. But it's a strange
feeling. In the moment, even now, I don't feel safe
at all, as if any second someone come through that
door and try to hurt me.

                 There is a knock at the door.

                 The two look at each other.

                 DR. FREDERICKS
I'm certain that whoever is behind that door, they
only have the best intentions for you. Come in.

                 NURSE KISSAM enters.

                 DR. FREDERICKS (Continued)
Yes, Nurse?

                    NURSE
There's someone to see you, Doctor.

                    DR. FREDERICKS
I'm in the middle of a session.

              The NURSE looks uncomfortable.

                    NURSE
We have a surprise visitor.

                    DR. FREDERICKS reads between the
                    lines.

                    DR. FREDERICKS
All right. Ms. Moll, would you please wait here in my
office. I won't be long.

                    NURSE KISSAM exits, but DR.
                    FREDERICKS stays at the door a
                    moment longer.

                    DR. FREDERICKS
I want you to think about what you read in that
newspaper, before getting on the freeway. Can you do
that for me?

                    AGATHA
It's not much of a memory.

                    DR. FREDERICKS
It's a start. I'll be back in a moment. Just be
calm. There's nothing to fear.

                    DR. FREDERICKS exits.

                    After a pause, AGATHA rises and
                    begins to look around the doctor's
                    office. She picks up books and
                    inspects things without purpose.

> She stands at one of the walls,
> staring at a plaque posted there.
>
> <u>Suddenly</u> – the wall moves
> backwards a few feet.
>
> AGATHA jumps!
>
> The wall holds. AGATHA reaches
> out her hand.
>
> The wall moves backward again.
>
> Then again.
>
> The voice of NANCY 1 and NANCY 2
> can be heard behind the wall.

                    NANCY 1
          (Off stage)
Someone is here to see you.

                    NANCY 2
          (Off stage)
He won't be let in. He'll try to sneak in later.

                    AGATHA
Who is it?

                    NANCY 1 | NANCY 2
          (Off stage)
Wouldn't you like to know?

                    AGATHA
Don't tease me.
          (No answer)
If you know you should tell me.

                    NANCY 2
          (Off stage)
It would just confuse you.

                    AGATHA
I'm already confused.

                    NANCY 1
          (Off stage)
You'll know soon enough.

                    The wall moves backwards again.

                    AGATHA
How are you doing that?

                    NANCY 1
          (Off stage)
There are secrets in this place. This is one of them.
The entire building can change shape. There are doors
where there once were none. There are closets where
before there was a sink. On some days—

                    NANCY 2
There is a basement. On other days—

                    NANCY 1
Nothing.

                    AGATHA
Lillian. She said there was a secret. Is that it?

                    NANCY 2
          (Off stage, breathy)
There is a secret bigger than this Hotel being alive.

                    The wall opens to reveal a black
                    room behind.

                    AGATHA looks behind her.

                    NANCY 1 | NANCY 2
Come and join us, sisssssster. We can help you find
your beautiful boyfriend Dean.

                    She considers.

> AGATHA

What if I say no?

> The wall moves back in a few
> inches, closer to its original
> position.

> AGATHA runs forward—

> AGATHA

No, no. Wait. Wait. This path leads to Dean.

> NANCY 1

Trust us.

> NANCY 2

Trust us.

> At last, AGATHA enters the void.

> The wall shuts behind her.

> Curtain.

ACT II

SCENE 1

DEAN FOSTER sits in a director's
chair in an open space.

Surrounding him, unidentifiable
FIGURES.

                    FOSTER
It happens. It's the business. People are fickle.
Tastes come and go. I don't like the decision, but
it's not one I can fight. After all, it's their
money. What's that? No. This is a first. I've
completed *every single picture* I've started. Never
had any complaints. Well, I suppose that's not true.
My shenanigans have been written up in the trades.
I've butted a few heads with the execs – well, one
exec in particular – but I thought we had moved past
all that. Nope – on time and on budget. There was no
apparent reason for the shutdown except that those in
power had a change of heart. Speak up a bit. That's
a great question. One that I asked straight out, soon
as I got the axe. To my knowledge, they're not
looking to recast. I don't think they had a problem
with either Rod or Agatha. Only me. Which is ironic
when you think about it. Because what you see on
film, even the things that they told me they like...
it's all me.

                    Blackout.

                    ACT II

                    SCENE 2

                    AGATHA rides FOSTER on the floor
                    in the furniture-less apartment.
                    He turns her over and, angrily,
                    thrusts into her. At last, he
                    relaxes and falls over her,
                    breathing heavy.

                    AGATHA
          (Breathing heavily)
Well... that was different.

                    FOSTER
How do you mean?

                    AGATHA
A little rough.

                    FOSTER
Sorry.

                    AGATHA
Something happen? You're not yourself.

                    FOSTER
Nothing.

                    He gets up, sweeps his clothes and
                    uses his shirt to towel the
                    perspiration from his chest.

                    FOSTER (Continued)
I need to wash up.

                    He exits to the bathroom.

                    SOUND: Water running.

                    AGATHA dresses.

                    FOSTER (Continued)
          (Off stage)
Your dad's a real prick, Shirley.

                    AGATHA

What did you say?

                    FOSTER
          (Off stage)
He fired me. Today. Last shot of the day was it for
me. I'm not back tomorrow. The production will shut
down for two weeks while they find my replacement.
They're making an announcement at call time tomorrow.
I've already given interviews.

                    AGATHA
Did you just call me Shirley?

                         Pause. FOSTER appears in the
                         bathroom doorway, toweling off his
                         face.

                    FOSTER
Well, that's your name, isn't it?

                    AGATHA

I'm Agatha.

                    FOSTER

Ok, sure.

                         He smiles and returns to the sink.

                    FOSTER (Continued)
          (Off stage)
You're as nutty as your daddy. The film's eighty
percent in the can. And he goes and cocks it up. You
know what he told me? He calls me up to his office
with that cold-ass secretary of his and says, "Mr.
Foster, I'm removing you from your current assignment.
The word's come down and it's final. We'll be
                    (MORE)

                                                    63

FOSTER (Continued)

assigning another director to take it from here and
making a full completion payment on your contract."
"That's it?" I say. "Just like that?" "Just like
that." And then he mumbled something about a witness,
like I had done something wrong. Something really
wrong. Not like just fucking his daughter. Like I
had been seen *in flagrante delicto*.
          (Pause)
But I don't know. It happened kinda fast. I should
have smashed his goddamn face. But I left. Hell,
Shirl, the press was waiting for me downstairs and I
had to play it all cool. It's just so fucking
embarrassing, you know! I've never, ever, ever, ever
been fired.

                    SOUND: The water shuts off.

                    He's again at the doorway, shirt
                    off. AGATHA stands opposite.
                    She's mute.

                    FOSTER (Continued)

What's the matter, Agatha? You look like you've seen
a ghost.

                    AGATHA

Agatha?

                    FOSTER

Well that's your name, isn't it?

                    AGATHA

Did you have an affair with Shirley Pendarsky?

                    FOSTER

That's a little private.
          (Pause)
So maybe I did.

                    AGATHA

Do you screw all your leading ladies?

FOSTER

Not when I did that horse picture. Shack up with a mare and the whole town gossips. I'm joking. What's wrong? Shirley and I are ancient history. Why you bringing this up now when it's going so good?

AGATHA

You told me just now you were fired today.

FOSTER

I hope not! I've just started casting. I don't want to get fired from two pictures in a row. Then I'd be dead meat. Never direct again. No, thank you. One time's enough.

>He crosses to her, tries to hug her, but she moves away.

FOSTER (Continued)

Tell me what I did and I'll fix it.

AGATHA

You called me Shirley.

FOSTER

What? No!

AGATHA

Just now?

FOSTER

I didn't even speak. Look, are you drunk? No more martinis—

AGATHA

You just told me about the day you were fired from *Beach Fun*.

FOSTER

Ah, you're tight.

>He waves her off and returns to the bathroom, shutting the door.

                    After a pause, there is a knock at
                    the other door. AGATHA startles.
                    Another bang, harder. AGATHA
                    looks to the bathroom. FOSTER
                    doesn't emerge.

                    The front door of the apartment
                    comes open by itself and hangs
                    there.

                    AGATHA walks to the opening and
                    peers outside.

                    AGATHA
            (Changing voice, tougher)
Are you coming in or are you just going to stand in
the hallway?

                    Hesitantly, RAY PENDARSKY enters.

                    He looks around the empty
                    apartment, hat in hand, surveying,
                    pacing.

                    RAY
Where is he?

                    AGATHA
He's not here.

                    RAY
Is this where he takes you?

                    AGATHA
He takes me lots of places.

                    RAY
I knew it had gotten bad. But I didn't know this bad.
I don't need to call a doctor, do I?

                    AGATHA
For what?

                    RAY

He hasn't gotten you pregnant?

                    AGATHA

Daddy. We're careful.

                    RAY
                (Smirks)
Careful. You mother said she was being careful, but
here I am... Look. You're nineteen. You can do what
you want. Screw it up. See if I care. I got you
what you wanted and this is how you repay me?

                    AGATHA

You don't know what I want.

                    RAY

I do. Or at least I thought I did. Look, kid.
Actress fall for their directors all the time. It
happens. You're not the first. And I can tell you...
it always ends like a damn train wreck.

                    AGATHA

I'm glad you still continue to know the outcome of
everything. If that were so true, you'd be doing
better at the box office.

                    RAY

Put it this way: it's like summer camp. You fall in
love, neck in the bushes, and it's all dangerous and
weird and surprising. But it's not love. Shirley.
It's not love.
                (Pause)
You'll see when the show's over. When that final
dialog recording is done and he's onto the next
project, his next leading lady... you'll know I'm
right.

                    AGATHA

It's important to be right.

                    RAY

No. It's important to be sane.

                         The bathroom door opens. Instead
                         of FOSTER, THE ORDERLY emerges.

He wears his white pants, but his
shirt is off and he's using it to
towel his face.

                    RAY (Continued)
Who the hell is this? Shirley. Who the hell is this?

THE ORDERLY comes forward, hand
outstretched.

                    THE ORDERLY
I'm a good friend. I'm fucking your daughter.

RAY backs away.

                    RAY
          (To AGATHA)
I don't know you anymore. You don't behave like this.
You don't have *men* like this. You're not my little
girl.

RAY exits.

THE ORDERLY goes and shuts the
door RAY left open.

When he turns, his face is
distorted, maniacal. He starts to
laugh.

AGATHA joins him, laughing and
crouching. The two move
strangely, laughing, until they
are in each other's arms. They
begin to ravage each other.

Lights fade.

ACT II

SCENE 3

DR. FREDERICKS and NURSE KISSAM,
in the doctor's office. They sit
very still, almost doll-like.

Enter THE ORDERLY.

As he enters, they turn their
heads and follow him slowly about
the room. He circles. He cups
their breasts, each, just for a
lingering second, then he leans
against the wall and lights a
cigarette.

                    THE ORDERLY
I've confirmed the matta'. Dean Foster's been kicked
off'a the movie. So that is that. Ray's found
someone new to take over. He's a Pollock. He's
shooting with that new girl Agatha Moll right now.
She's cute. You'd like her. A lot. Maybe we'll get
a chance to meet her someday. You can keep playing
your parts, good as you do.
          (Pause)
Look, I know you think... well, you think I'm taking a
lot of chances lately, but... I just want you to know
I've, I've never felt better about things. For once,
I kinda feel good about the way things is going. This
place can get a man down. Like I'm pinned under a
truck that's turned over on the highway, and I'm
screamin', screamin', "Help, help! Come and, and pull
my arm, and..."
          (Pause)
You two is a bad influence. Yeah, I know what you're
thinking. I'm the influence. Man, I know about
influences. But before I got here, I was into more
than makin' mischief. I wanted to really take over
the world! Now I just want everything to, to turn out
the way it oughta. The way it's all lined up ta be.
It's like a work of freaking art.

He turns, eyes the two women.

THE ORDERLY
Look at you. Like in a painting. Don't let your oils
run. Daddy's here...

He moves in.

Lights fade.

ACT II

SCENE 4

A cluster of female PATIENTS in
the day room surrounds LILLIAN,
who gossips in a whisper.

Enter AGATHA.

LILLIAN shoves away the others
when she sees THE ORDERLY cross
into the room.

THE ORDERLY spots her and ambles
over.

                    THE ORDERLY
Hey.

                    LILLIAN
Hey.

                    THE ORDERLY
Long time.

                    LILLIAN
No see.

                    THE ORDERLY
I've been busy.

                    LILLIAN
Oh?

                    THE ORDERLY
You don't want to know all the dirty details.

He shuffles next to her, real
close.

                    LILLIAN
I've been busy, too.

                          THE ORDERLY
You know I rely on you from time ta time. You're good
in a corner. I like that about you. Ya don't
complain much neither.

                          LILLIAN
I'm made to take direction.

                          THE ORDERLY
I bet you are.

                    He caresses her hair.

                          THE ORDERLY (Continued)
That dress looks good on you.

                          LILLIAN
Why, thank you.

                          THE ORDERLY
You remember the plan, don't you? I've made a change.
Shouldn't be too hard to wrap your head around. Why
don't I come to your room tonight and insert where
required?

                          LILLIAN
You're the Devil.

                          THE ORDERLY
No, but we do run in the same social circles. So I
can come 'round?

                          LILLIAN
Okay.

                          THE ORDERLY
Okay? That's it?

                          LILLIAN
Okay.

                    THE ORDERLY shrugs, bemused.

                    THE ORDERLY
Why you wanna be my friend, Lil?

                    LILLIAN
Don't you know? I'm using you.

                    THE ORDERLY
          (Smiling)
Oh, really? Is that the truth?

                    Dismissive, he breaks away and
                    smacks her rear.

                    THE ORDERLY
See you tonight.

                    THE ORDERLY crosses and exits,
                    cutting a swath through the
                    PATIENTS.

                    After a pause, NURSE KISSAM enters
                    with AGATHA. The NURSE drops her
                    off in the room and exits.

                    LILLIAN
Agatha! Come here!

                    AGATHA
I'm tired. I don't want to talk.

                    LILLIAN
That's the drugs.

                    AGATHA
I'm not taking any drugs.

                    LILLIAN
Oh, yes you are. It's in the air. Wafts through the
ducts like a fog.

                    AGATHA
Have you been diagnosed with paranoia, Lillian?

LILLIAN

I have a long list of ailments, starting with you. I
want to hear your explanation. Who told you? How do
you know?

AGATHA

What are you talking a—?

LILLIAN

Was it him? Did he tell you? The other night. So
cruel. You say you know the name of the witness.
Are you lying? After I gave it thought, that was my
conclusion. You've been here too short a time to
discover anything.

AGATHA

Is this a confession that you were listening at my
door the other night? Should I report you to the
orderly?

LILLIAN

Don't you wonder how I get to move about? Don't you
wonder where I go from time to time, when you don't
see me?

AGATHA

No. What I wonder about is why you get to wear a
yellow dress when our mouths are stuffed with white?
I can't imagine that orderly let you skirt the rules
without some little taste. Someone told me you're a
lesbian.

LILLIAN

Someone told me it doesn't matter. The focus is on
you. I'm the most *human* thing in this hotel and don't
think for a second, one *second* that I don't prize that
very highly. You should be nicer to me. I can do
things for you. I've been here longer than any of the
others. I know all the ins and outs.

AGATHA

Do you know about the secret passageway from Dr.
Frederick's office?
          (Pause)
Cat got your tongue?

                    LILLIAN
Who showed you that?

                    AGATHA
I found it myself. It leads outside of the grounds.

                    LILLIAN
Did you go out?

                    AGATHA
No. I didn't. I didn't have much time.

                    LILLIAN
You're a patient here. You have nothing but time.

                    AGATHA
Maybe one day I'll go missing and no one will be able
to find me.

                    LILLIAN
I don't think that's what you want. You want to be
found.
          (Pause)
You didn't answer. Don't you want to know... where
I've been..?

                    AGATHA
You've been with him. He's your lover, isn't he?
That's why you get the special privileges, know how to
get out of The Hotel, get to wear your own dress, know
the *secret* secret of this place.

                    LILLIAN
Sounds like you are right behind me on most counts.
Do you want a yellow dress, too? Or perhaps a blood
red one? You know the name now, so you say, so figure
it out yourself.
          (Moving in)
I want to play a little game. Will you do that?

                    AGATHA
I hate games.

                    LILLIAN
Look...

                                                    75

                              She points to the other PATIENTS
                              in the room. While they were
                              speaking, all have turned their
                              backs turned to LILLIAN and
                              AGATHA.

                    LILLIAN (Continued)
One of these patients is not what she seems. If you
pick the right one, you'll have a nice shock. If you
pick the wrong one, status quo. Do you want to see
what's real?

                    AGATHA
I. Hate. Games.

                    LILLIAN
But this is a good one.
          (Long pause)
Last chance. You won't regret it.

                              AGATHA, half-heartedly, picks out
                              a PATIENT.

                              The PATIENT turns. She's wearing
                              a mask, one different from the two
                              NANCYs, but one that robs her of
                              her features.

                    AGATHA
Why is she wearing that?

                    LILLIAN
That's her face.

                    AGATHA
But it a—?

                    LILLIAN
Pick another.

                              AGATHA gestures to another
                              PATIENT, who turns, with no

> indication how she knows she was
> the patient who was chosen.
>
> Again, the PATIENT wears a mask.

LILLIAN (Continued)
Third time is the charm.

> AGATHA, spellbound, slowly raising
> her finger and pointing to one
> more candidate.
>
> When this patient turns, it is
> DEAN FOSTER.
>
> AGATHA races to him.

AGATHA
Oh, Dean, I thought, I thought— How did you get here?

> FOSTER hugs AGATHA. Slowly, the
> remaining PATIENTS turn towards
> the lovers. They all wear masks.

LILLIAN
(Satisfied)
Good game.

> After a moment of affection
> between AGATHA and DEAN, she looks
> away.

AGATHA
Speak, Dean! Is it really you?

FOSTER
It is.

AGATHA

Well, how, how—?

FOSTER

Calm down. Lillian arranged it. She phoned me and
told me you were checked in here, and gave me
directions, and met me at the passageway, and, well...

AGATHA
                (Joyous)
I don't believe it! I don't believe it!

FOSTER

You didn't think I'd let you rot in a place like this,
did you? When I found out you were here, I got so
angry. Keeping you in here just to shut you up. It's
not right! What kind of—?

AGATHA

There's nothing wrong with me. There's nothing wrong
with me.

FOSTER

I know that, doll. You're perfect. Perfect.

                     They kiss. As they do, the others
                     exit slowly.

                     FOSTER (Continued)

Look, I've got some bad news.

AGATHA

No news can dampen me. You're here!

FOSTER

They've... recast the part. It's going forward with
another girl. She's your father's secretary. I
didn't approve. I fought it. Hard. But, Christ,
Shirley, he gave me no choice.

AGATHA
                (Stunned)
What did you say?

FOSTER

We start up in ten days. She's already had her
wardrobe fitted. She's a sweet girl, she really is.
But she can't act. She's a virgin. No, I, I don't
mean in that way - I mean never been in a picture
before. You would have creamed her. I tried to stall
them as long as I could, rejecting every actress they
threw at me. But you know how these things go, Shirl.
Great, big machines and a little guy like me can't
stop them.

AGATHA

My name is *Agatha*.

FOSTER

What?

AGATHA

My name is Agatha Moll.

FOSTER

No. That's her name. The actress who replaced you in
the picture. Did someone tell you this already? Did
you sneak in a newspaper or something?

AGATHA

No, Dean! *I* am Agatha! I'm Agatha Moll!

FOSTER

Calm *down*, Shirley.

AGATHA

Shirley Pendarsky disappeared. You told me that the
last time I saw you. You said that you knew something
about her from Ray Pendarsky, but you wouldn't tell me
what it was. You were going to set it all right. You
left me on the lot and didn't say anything more, but
you, you were strange that night. I could tell. You
were disturbed. And the next morning, it was in the
papers. That you were dead. You were found dead.
"Film Director Dies in Accident" and it had your
photograph. And I decided, that, that I had *no other
choice*, but to come here, because that's the only part
you told me. You said that Shirley Pendarsky was no
longer in the hospital. I knew the address. I knew
because *I was his secretary, Dean*.

                         FOSTER
Stop talking. I'm clearly not dead.

                         AGATHA
I know, I know. People don't talk much around the
dead. Especially with their mouths. It was Nancy who
told me you were alive. She was right. You aren't
dead after all.

                         FOSTER
Nancy. Who's Nancy?

                         AGATHA
My sister.

                         FOSTER
You don't have a sister.

                         AGATHA
Agatha Moll's sister!

                         FOSTER
You sure know a lot about Agatha Moll.

                         AGATHA
Because she's me, Dean! Jesus Christ, don't you—?

                         FOSTER
Shirley. I don't know what you're talking about. But
it's scaring me. I thought you being committed as a
cruel trick of your father's. People think I'm a
jerk, but he's... you don't lock up your daughter for
falling in love with her director. I came to get you
out. Either I was going to sneak you out that
passageway, or I was going to sign you out legit.
          (Pause)
But all this you're saying...

                         AGATHA
The papers were wrong. You're alive, but, but you've
got something into your head, Dean. Did you get in an
accident? Did you lose your memory? Do you not
recognize my face? We've been lovers for two months.
Since that day you saw me in water. How do I know all
this if I'm Shirley; how do I know all this if it
hasn't happened yet?

FOSTER

I'm getting help.

FOSTER debates. AGATHA weeps.

AGATHA
(Hysterical)
Don't go, Dean. Stay with me. Don't leave me!

FOSTER
I'm getting help! I'm getting help!

He pushes her away, roughly, and
then exits quickly.

Lights flare behind the walls.

NANCY 1 and NANCY 2 are buried in
the scrims.

NANCY 1

You've done it now.

NANCY 2

You can't stop them.

NANCY 1
They're onto you. He'll be back with a whole mess of
trouble for our little sister.

AGATHA
Sister! Sister! Yes, yes. You're my dead sister
Nancy. You're Nancy. You're both Nancy. And if
you're my sister, I'm Agatha. You prove it. Don't
leave. Stay. Tell them who I am. Tell them who I
am!

Lights behind the scrims fade and
AGATHA screams just as THE
ORDERLY, with DR. FREDERICKS,
NURSE KISSAM, LILLIAN, and FOSTER
re-enter.

                         THE ORDERY is the first and he
                         roughly holds AGATHA, who writhes
                         and screams at the top of her
                         lungs.

                         THE ORDERLY
It's the shocks for her, Doctor. You can see it's
time, like I been tellin' ya.

                         DR. FREDERICKS
I'll decide when it's time.
              (To FOSTER)
How long has she been like this?

                         FOSTER
Just a few minutes. She's thinks she's someone else.

                         LILLIAN
She's been erratic all day, Doctor. I tried to settle
her, but it was no good.

                         AGATHA
I'm not crazy! I'm Agatha.

                         DR. FREDERICKS
Shirley, please calm down. You'll give us no choice.

                         AGATHA
You gave me treatment, Doctor! I told you about my
sister Nancy. You know who I am. You know who I am!
Tell me who I am!

                         She's out of control. THE ORDERLY
                         binds her arms with his grip and
                         carries her out of the room.

                         DR. FREDERICKS
              (To FOSTER)

This is why we don't have *visitors*, Mr. Foster. It
upsets them. Now I want you to leave immediately. I
don't know who snuck you in here or how, but we have a
strict policy. Get out. She's in good hands.

                    DR. FREDERICKS exits. NURSE
                    KISSAM turns to follow, but FOSTER
                    catches her arm.

                    DR. FREDERICKS (Continued)
          (To NURSE)
What are they going to do to her?

                    NURSE
We have a treatment. I'll be back to show you out in
a moment. You shouldn't have come, Mr. Foster. You
should have listened to us and stayed away. Whoever
snuck you in... did the wrong thing. Please wait here
until I come and get you.

                    The NURSE exits.

                    LILLIAN and FOSTER stare at each
                    other.

                    FOSTER
Why didn't you tell me she was so bad off? You sneak
out, make me a rescuer. What's wrong with you? She
needs this place.

                    LILLIAN
I'll watch out for her. I do like her. And I want
her to be well. We have a lot in common. I'm an
actress, too.

                    FOSTER
Great! Another crazy fucking actress.

                    LILLIAN

Got a part for me in your picture? I'm very good.
Very, very, very good... with parts.

                    LILLIAN slithers up to FOSTER.

                FOSTER
Give it a rest.

                    She moves even closer, touching
                    his inseam.

                LILLIAN
     (Soft)
What if I told you she was right... that you are going
to die? Would that scare you?

                FOSTER
She's been jabbering about that to you, too? That
story about me in the papers? "Film Director Dies in
Accident." Don't believe a word of it.

                LILLIAN
     (Soft)
But you should. I saw it happen. I am *the witness*.

                Blackout.

ACT II

SCENE 5

The shock room.

AGATHA receives brutal shock
treatments.

ACT II

SCENE 6

AGATHA's room at The Hotel.

AGATHA lays on her bed, calm,
under covers that go up to her
eyeballs.

Beside her, seated on a chair, is
THE ORDERLY.

                    THE ORDERLY
You have a great face. I'm sorry we broke a few blood
vessels. You'll understand more in a coupla hours.
This place is built to house delusions. Not necessary
to house the delusional. There's a' difference, you
know? I like to think of this ol' Hotel as collecting
all the rage, disappointment, fear, let-downs, come-
downs, come-ons, and despair that this town grows in
its garden. Hell, gardens all over the Midwest, big
fertile gardens. I've been out there, you know? I've
been all over. I love those farm girls. Those girls
wit' the big eyes and curves who get stared at by
everyone in the corner store and know, know, know for
certain, deep down, that they're too pretty for that
farm. They need to be shared with everybody. Passed
'round like a bottle of whiskey at a hobo rail-yard
bonfire. I'd like to think (and so would their
mothers and fathers, I bet) that these girls have
talent and want to share that talent with the rest of
the world. But it's more physical than that. It
ain't about sharing talent. It's about just plain
exposure. You've got to be seen. You've got to be of
consequence. And Hollywood, for all its wrecks and
its poisons and its drift... one thing it does have is
plenty of opportunity to be noticed. For the bad shit
as much as the good. And all this applies to the
boys, too. They're no better. They don't get off any
lighter.
          (Pause)
I betcha I could get noticed. I have some powers.
You look like you don't believe me. I'm more than an
orderly at a lousy sanitarium. I've got connections;
                    (MORE)

THE ORDERLY (Continued)
I get orders, sure, but I give 'em, in this world and
the next. I'm not someone's dog.
          (Considering)
Well, if I am... I'm one that can bite your face off.

                    AGATHA starts to take off her
                    covers. THE ORDERLY sets them
                    right and tucks her in so tightly
                    she can't move.

          THE ORDERLY (Continued)
Go to sleep. I won't touch you. I've got a date,
anyways. What's that look you're giving me? Is that
disappointment? Does baby want some? Or is that look
'cos you're scared to be alone? You'll even take me
over the empty room.

              THE ORDERLY stands.

          THE ORDERLY (Continued)
Do you want to see your sister? Yeah, that's right.
Do you want to see your Nancy? Two cracked little
dolls, each with half a head. The dead twins you
remember, but remember all wrong. I could call 'em,
with a snap. Call 'em. Just a snap. Want me to do
it? It looks like you need a break. And I've got
plans. I'll have to send out the ding-a-ling, yoo-hoo
for them another night.

              He opens the door to leave.

          THE ORDERLY (Continued)
Tell you what. I'll do you a favor. You're pissed at
that Foster now for calling in reinforcements. I can
understand that. I'll do you one right. When he gets
going on his movie, I'm going to get him fired. And
then, you know what I'll do? I'll fucking kill him
and make it look like an accident. Would that make

you happy, Agatha? Or Shirley? Or whoever the hell
you want to be...

> He slams of the door.

> Lights fade.

ACT II

SCENE 7

RAY PENDARSKY's office.

RAY and FOSTER sit across from
each other.

                    RAY
I'm as surprised as you are. I didn't think you'd
come. We left this peach a little bruised.

                    FOSTER
Technically, I'm still under contract to the studio.

                    RAY
Business. That's why you came? I saw some of the
rushes from your latest. Not bad. Funny. I hope you
keep the bit in with the moving staircase. That was
good. How did you get the steps to do that?

                    FOSTER
Lots of union guys.

                    RAY
Ah. Of course. Well... it was funny. I hope when
it's all cut together that it does good box office and
we can put that whole beach picture business behind
us. I think Ryczyk did a good job picking up for you,
but I've always wondered what the end result would
have been if it was *you* who had finished the shooting,
and the cut, the print, et cetera.

                    FOSTER
I would have liked to have seen it through, too. It
was coming together. Coming together.

                    RAY
Don't think I don't have regrets about our decision,
Dean. I was under tremendous pressure from forces you
don't understand. It was strictly—

                    FOSTER
I know Hollywood. You're in; you're out. In and out.
It's how this town functions. I'm not bitter. At
least not about that.

                    RAY
All right. Now I see. And this is a good transition
to why you are here.

                         RAY pulls a memo from his desk and
                         hands it to FOSTER.

                         FOSTER reads. When he's done, he
                         looks a little stunned. He sets
                         the memo back down on the desk.

                    FOSTER
Is that true?

                    RAY
What do you think?

                    FOSTER
Lots of memos come out of your office. Not all of
them are true.

                    RAY
This one is. Everything in there.

                    FOSTER
Do you really think she'll show up on the lot?

                    RAY
No. But I needed to take precautions. Shirley could
have gone anywhere. Hell, she could be headed to
Broadway, start a new career as a chorus girl.

                    FOSTER
You don't really think that.

                    RAY
I thought she was improving. She'd been receiving
treatments and, from my last report from Dr.
Fredericks, she was doing better.

FOSTER

I'm glad for that.

RAY

But something told me the reports were lies. I don't
like the caliber of employees at that hospital. I
wanted to ask a few questions. So I went to see her.
When I arrived, that Dr. Fredericks wouldn't let me
see my little girl. Said she was in a state. Not a
very... clinical... appraisal. I thought I had full
rights to visit her—

FOSTER

Though you rarely did.

RAY
            (Agreeing)
Though I rarely did. A nurse stopped me in the lobby.
She called the doctor who told me Shirley had
deteriorated over the past several days and was, at
that moment, in a session and it... would... be... *bad*
for me to see her.

FOSTER

That is that.

RAY

But again, I didn't believe them. So I left. And I
circled the building on foot. And I got mud on my
shoes—

FOSTER

Poor baby.

RAY

It was a wet day and there was that ivy, covering
everything, and the hedges, and the red brick of the
place. I couldn't see in any of the widows. They
were all boarded or fogged. And high. I'm not that
tall. I looked a little ridiculous jumping at
windows, in the misty rain, in mud, in my suit and
necktie, hoping to catch a glimpse of a daughter that
long ago left me. But I kept looking. And the more I
was in a proximity to that place... the more I kept,
kept walking in its presence, the more... The place
just gave me... the most horrid feeling. Like it
was...

                    FOSTER
I've never told you this. But I visited Shirley. One
time, a few months back.

                    RAY
Oh?

                    FOSTER
She was worse than I could have imagined. I think she
had split personality or something.

                    RAY
She's never been diagnosed with that.

                    FOSTER
I'm no doctor. What I mean to say is: what she told
me, and the way she behaved... That wasn't Shirley.
Not the Shirley I knew. Oh, sure, there were
glimpses. But that was all. But I'm telling you
this, not to make you mad, you see. I know you didn't
like her and I seeing each other, thought it would be
bad for her career and the picture and for you and all
that jazz. I'm telling you this because I felt it,
too. But never said anything. That place...

                    RAY
That place...

                    FOSTER
The place she's now vanished from.

                    RAY
Is not a hospital.

                    FOSTER
It's not. I even feel, real deep down in my stomach,
that that place not even be a real building.
          (Pause)
You never saw the place before checking her in?

                    RAY
No. It was recommended by a producer I know. Small
time fellow. Good man; I'd trust him.

                    FOSTER
Trust him with your daughter?

                    RAY

I did.

                    FOSTER

Where is he now?
          (Pause, no answer)
I bet you didn't even drive her out there. I can tell
by your face that that's right. Probably had your
secretary do it. Why you put Shirley in that
hospital, Ray? Was it because I was sleeping with
her?

                    RAY

I didn't like you. I never liked you. But I didn't
put her away because of you. I'm not a monster. She,
she... She started saying all sorts of foul things.
Lies. They'd just come out. Did she ever do that
around you? She'd just lie and lie. And she told me
she'd, she'd go to the papers with these lies and I
knew that she was better away, somewhere quiet, for
just a little while. Until she was better. I'd
rather have here somewhere safe than saying things at
parties and to reporters or anyone who would listen to
gossip and consider printing it, unsubstantiated. It
was just rambling. A little rebellious teenage girl.
I didn't think it would be forever. You know *this
town*, Dean. Grrr! This town! Can't give you a
break; can't take a moment to find out the truth.

                    FOSTER

What is the truth, Ray?

                    RAY

That she was my daughter! And that she had some
problems. And I wanted to get her some goddamn help.

                    FOSTER

Quiet help.

                    RAY

Don't - don't look at me like that. This wasn't a
snuff job. This was and *is*: my daughter. My daughter
who is missing.

FOSTER
(Lazy)
So you put out a memo to all the gates and building
chiefs to be on the lookout, that she might try to
charm her way in, and that she had friends here, but
that she wasn't to be allowed on the lot and that, if
anyone saw her, to call Ray Pendarsky's office, day or
night. Whose phone number is on there? Yours at home
or that redhead out front? All right, I get it. I
get it. You invited me to your office not for
business. But because you wanted me to know she,
what, escaped from the hospital and she might try to
contact me? That it? And if I see her I, what?, try
to get her to come to you, or drive her back to that
place—?

RAY
No. She's not going back. Now that she's out, I want
her out. I don't like the people there, not a one,
not a one. I would have gotten her out sooner if I
didn't think it would disrupt the treatments.
Whatever they thought was working was not. They've
failed her. She's out by her own accord and I'll find
her a better way.

FOSTER
But you're going to send her somewhere.

RAY
I'm not sure what I'm going to do! I, I don't think
that far ahead when it comes to Shirley, Dean. I've
made a lot of mistakes as a father. I don't think. I
don't think. Now I'm asking you for *help*. You don't
owe me a thing, nothing. Nothing. But you are
Shirley were an item. The last item before putting
her in that place and I think she'll go to you first.

FOSTER
Do you know a girl named Lillian?

RAY
I probably know a few Lillians.

FOSTER
She is a patient with Shirley. She snuck me in the
(MORE)

FOSTER (Continued)

time I visited; they stopped me in the lobby, too, but
then I had a little help. As I was leaving, Lillian
told me something I didn't understand at the time.
Something about a witness. Then, when you fired me
from Beach Fun, you said you knew the witness.

RAY

I did? Strange thing to say.

FOSTER

Yes, I thought so, too.
          (Pause)
Witness to what?

RAY

I don't remember.

FOSTER

No, no. You were very clear about it. You told me I
was out and that you knew this witness. I figured it
was something about Agatha Moll. That you had someone
spying on us.

RAY

Should I have been spying on you?

FOSTER

No. I still thought I was being fired as payback for
Shirley. Not only did you not like me dating Shirley,
you hated it even worse that I was seeing Agatha Moll.
But, too late, I remembered Lillian's comment. She
was to be a witness to something very important.
          (Pause)
What did you mean, Ray, about the witness?

RAY

I don't know what you're talking about. I don't know
any nuts named Lillian. We're talking about Shirley
here. Let's keep our focus. Will you help me, Dean?
Will you help me put Shirley on the right path? I
know that she'll come to you. She'll find you. And
when she does... call me. Day or night.

Lights fade.

ACT II

SCENE 8

FOSTER's empty apartment.

FOSTER enters the dark room, looks
about. He notices a light under
the bathroom door.

He approaches the door, resigned.
He lifts his hand to knock, but
then lets it drop.

                    FOSTER
Shirley? Is that you?
          (No answer)
I know you still have your key.
          (Pause)
Come out. I want to speak with you.
          (Pause)
It's okay. It's going to be fine. I want to help
you, in any way I can.
          (Pause)
Just tell me what you want.

                    FOSTER surrenders and steps from
                    the door.

                    FOSTER (Continued)
It's all right. I'll wait as long as you want me to.

                    After a long pause, the door
                    opens, so slowly and quietly that
                    FOSTER does not notice, or turn.

                    A WOMAN IN MASK stands in the
                    doorway. It is the same mask the
                    PATIENTS wore before. She wears a
                    blood red dress.

                    FOSTER talks into the floor.

FOSTER (Continued)
Your father told me that you got out. That you'd try
to find me. I came here, because I know it's the only
place that you'd find safe. The last time we spoke,
it didn't go as I wanted. I know that I was...
severe. I want you know that your father has given me
his word that he won't send you back to that place
ever again.

> The WOMAN IN MASK eases forward,
> closer, closer, as he speaks.

FOSTER (Continued)
Come out. My car is downstairs. We can take the
Freeway, go anywhere you want. I've got a full tank
of gas and my driver has the night off. Anywhere in
L.A. My treat. And then, when you've had enough,
I'll take you home and we'll figure this out.

> The WOMAN IN MASK reveals a
> straight razor. Raising it, she
> lurches at FOSTER just as he
> turns.
>
> Before he has a chance to react,
> she slashes him to death and
> leaves him dead on the floor.
>
> As the lights fade, she takes off
> her mask.
>
> It's LILLIAN.
>
> Blackout.

ACT II

SCENE 9

LILLIAN stands an open space.

Surrounding her, unidentifiable
FIGURES.

                    LILLIAN
How does it feel to be me? What a fantastic question!
It feels amazing. You know, I'm just a simple
California girl who was lucky to go this far in life.
To have had two box office successes in a row, well I
never would have imagined. Sure, my father was in the
business, but I've made my own breaks. I always had
to work and struggle, just like any young actress in
Hollywood. You pay your dues. What's that? Well
there's a name! I haven't heard his name spoken in a
year or more. Yes, I had dinner with Dean Foster on a
few occasions, but I hardly think it was serious. We
weren't steadies or anything. No, I enjoyed the man's
company and I like to think he enjoyed mine, despite
rumors that I'm no fan of men. Men of his sort, I
mean. Yes, I was sad to hear about his accident. The
L.A. freeway is a danger and there are many, many
twists and turns. It's like one of our own movies –
you never know what's going to happen and who might
end up on top. For example, that business of my
father being involved somehow. Rubbish. My father
liked Dean very much. Dean was known to like women
and women liked Dean and I must confess that I was one
of those women. He had a reputation for being a lion,
but he was really ever so sweet to me, a gentle little
lamb who left this life too soon. Oh! Really! You
do like to pull names out of hats like little white
rabbits. I haven't seen her in a very long time.
Yes, I knew her socially before I was cast in her now-
vacant part, but we were not close. I wish Agatha
Moll all the best in the world, wherever she may be.
She was the sweetest little thing.

                    Blackout.

ACT II

SCENE 10

The Hotel, main room.

SOUND: A loud mechanical blur.

Lights fade in on AGATHA. She is
in The Hotel, surrounded by
PATIENTS. She alone wears a
yellow dress.

Music plays – a docile lullaby,
faraway.

THE ORDERY enters, passes through,
lingers near AGATHA. As she
stands there, aimless, he comes
behind her and puts his hands on
her, smiles.

                    THE ORDERLY
          (Hard to hear over the sound)
I'm glad you're here to stay. I like you. I always
have liked you.

THE ORDERLY smiles again and
exits.

DR. FREDERICKS and NURSE KISSAM
pass through, inhuman, robotic.

After a silent pause, AGATHA
screams.

ALL but AGATHA fall to the ground,
as if quickly melting into the
floor, where they lay in piles.

AGATHA stumbles around the bodies.

A spotlight strikes the corner,
where NANCY 1 and NANCY 2 stand.

                         Long pause.

                         AGATHA
                   (Screaming, shrill)
What is this plaaaaaaaaaaaaceeeee?????????

                         SOUND: The blur stops.

                         For a long moment, the room does
                         not answer, until:

                         NANCY 1
It's—

                         NANCY 2
Hollywood.

                         Blackout.

                         Final Curtain.

DESPERATE DOLLS

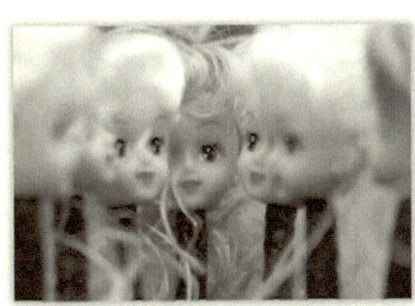

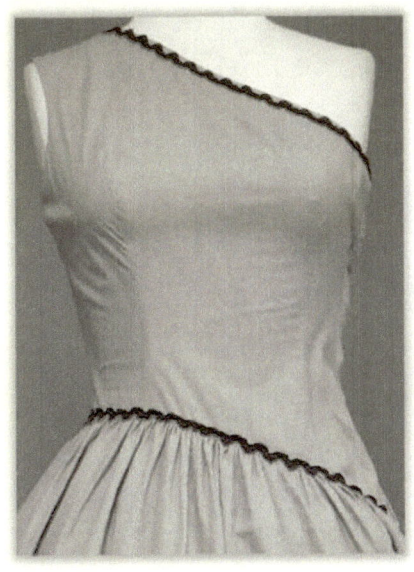

CAST OF CHARACTERS (in order of appearance)

    MATCHBOX, a young woman

    THE VIL (also known as "VIL"), a young woman

    PRETTY SEXY, a young woman

    CAPTAIN, an older man

    SUNNY JACK, an older man

THE SETTING

    Hollywood, California. Late 1960s.

THE SCENE

    A motel room that also doubles as an office, with one entry door, one bathroom door, a filing cabinet, a telephone, and a double-bed.

A NOTE ON MEDIA AND EFFECTS

    The motel room should be able to change appearance through light and other effects. Meaning, sometimes it will be bright and perfectly livable, other times a dingy hovel, while remaining the same static set.

    Sound design has a featured presence in the script and these have been indicated by "SOUND:" proceeding, for ease of review. Some sound effects are practical, others recorded.

    Photographs and flashes are used to represent filmed media, but it is the director's discretion on the best approach.

ACT I

SCENE 1

MATCHBOX, an attractive young
woman dressed in revealing
nightclothes, lies on a bed in a
darkened motel room. Above her, a
mirror hangs. The reflection
makes her look oddly distorted and
more visible to the audience.

                    MATCHBOX
Look at you. You pathetic bitch. Look at you.

          She opens then closes her legs.

                    MATCHBOX (Continued)
You'd like that. Wouldn't you? Look at you. You're
as bad as the rest.

          SOUND: A knock on the door.

          MATCHBOX covers her exposed body
          with the white sheet.

                    MATCHBOX (Continued)
Come...

          The door opens by itself. No one
          enters.

          After a pause, MATCHBOX sits up,
          holding the sheet in place.

                    MATCHBOX (Continued)
Is that you? Captain? Is that you?

>   She rises, wraps the sheet around
>   her shoulders, goes to the door,
>   and slowly shuts it.
>
>   SOUND: Another knock.
>
>
>   MATCHBOX (Continued)
>   (To door, in whisper)
> Is that you?
>
>
>   Lights fade.

ACT I

SCENE 2

Lights rise.

THE VIL (VIL) is on the bed,
alone, sleeping on the covers.
She is beautiful and wears a black
cocktail dress.

MATCHBOX is behind the bed now.
Only the top of her is visible.
She looks wild in her eyes.

THE VIL awakens and looks into the
overhead mirror, stretches.

She sees MATCHBOX's reflection in
the mirror. She startles! But
stays put on the bed.

                    THE VIL
You're back.

                    MATCHBOX
          (Cowering, scared)
He's here.

                    THE VIL
He can't be. You know that.

                    MATCHBOX
He's here.

                    THE VIL
Captain. He's here? You know that's impossible.

                    MATCHBOX
He's. Here.

                    THE VIL
Where?

                    MATCHBOX
He's in the lobby... and he's waiting for you. Just
like he waited for me.

                         MATCHBOX comes out, moving
                         strangely inhuman, snake-like.

                         THE VIL curls on the bed.

                    THE VIL
You need to go away. I don't like seeing you.

                    MATCHBOX
Get off. The bed.

                         THE VIL
No.

                    MATCHBOX
Are you scared of me? Don't be. I came to warn you.

                    THE VIL
How did you find me?

                    MATCHBOX
One motel room is quite like another. He's downstairs
waiting. He knows you have to leave sometime.

                    THE VIL
Jack's coming to rescue me.

                    MATCHBOX
Are you sure? He didn't rescue *me*. He didn't do
anything.

                    THE VIL
Jack loves me.

                    MATCHBOX
Are you absolutely *certain*?

                    MATCHBOX disappears.

THE VIL stays in a curl. She
spots her bathrobe across the
room. Her teeth chatter.
Quickly, she races to the hanger,
grabs the robe, runs back to the
bed, just in time for—

SOUND: Knock at the door.

                    THE VIL
          (Soft)
Come in.

The door opens slowly.

No one is there.

Lights fade.

ACT I

SCENE 3

SOUND: A retro bubblegum pop song
plays loudly, distorted, as if
through terrible loudspeakers.

Strobe lights begin.

The motel room is empty.

Enter PRETTY SEXY, an equivalent
beauty to the others, but
different. She wears a short
skirt and tight sweater.

PRETTY SEXY trembles in the
strobe, oddly moving and
frightened. She gropes the wall
and furniture, blinded.

                    PRETTY SEXY
              (Screaming over music)
     Jack! JACK! Help me, Jack!

Sudden blackness and silence.

ACT I

SCENE 4

Lights rise on SUNNY JACK, alone.

He knots a necktie. Finished, he grins and then bends to check himself in the mirror.

Meticulously, he arranges two folding chairs to facing.

Satisfied, he goes to the door and opens it.

                    SUNNY JACK
          (Calling offstage)
You can send the first one in now, Paul!

                    SUNNY JACK bobs back, slicks his
                    hair, and then waits.

                    MATCHBOX enters slowly, but with
                    confidence. She wears a happy
                    sundress, carries a small handbag,
                    and holds a large manila envelope.

                    SUNNY JACK (Continued)
Have a seat.

                    MATCHBOX sits in one of the
                    chairs. SUNNY JACK does *not* take
                    the opposite chair.

                    SUNNY JACK (Continued)
Let me see that.

                    MATCHBOX hands over the envelope.
                    SUNNY JACK examines the contents –
                    an actor's resume and headshot.

> He reads in silence, at last
> pointing to something on the
> resume.

SUNNY JACK (Continued)
You know I'm never going to remember that.

MATCHBOX
My name?

SUNNY JACK
Have you thought about changing it?

MATCHBOX
What's wrong with my name?

SUNNY JACK
Too... Anyway, you should change it.

MATCHBOX
(Doubtful)
I'll think about it.

SUNNY JACK
Says here you were in your high school's production of
Annie Get Your Gun. But it doesn't say who you
played.

MATCHBOX
Annie.

SUNNY JACK
Then say that.

> SUNNY JACK finally takes the
> second chair and hands her back
> the materials.

SUNNY JACK
You had any work in L.A.?

MATCHBOX
I've just arrived.

                    SUNNY JACK
Just?

                    MATCHBOX
Last week. Tuesday.

                    SUNNY JACK
Green. Who got you this audition?

                    MATCHBOX
Someone on the street. Said he worked for you. Paul.

                    SUNNY JACK
Did you recognize my name when he said it? Any of the
pictures I've done?

                    MATCHBOX
No, we didn't talk about you. He gave me a card with
your production company name on it. Though he said he
worked for someone important.

                    SUNNY JACK
I am important. I'm a triple threat. Producer,
director, writer. I'm probably better at the first
one than the others, but I'm not trying to win an
award.

                    MATCHBOX
Paul just said that he liked my face and, if I wanted
to, if I thought I could cut it, I could come here
this afternoon at 1 PM, and that you would give me a
shot.

                    SUNNY JACK
Were you worried I make dirty pictures?

                    MATCHBOX
Do you?

                    SUNNY JACK
          (Smiling)
Not anymore.
          (Pause)
I'm joking. You should laugh.

                    MATCHBOX
Like I said: Paul gave me a card. I figured producers
for obscene films wouldn't carry cards.

                    SUNNY JACK
You'd be right. They carry guns.

                    MATCHBOX
I'm not scared of guns.

                    SUNNY JACK
Of course. You were Annie.
          (Pause)
Twenty-six other girls are in that lobby. Not all of
them Paul met on the street. Some are from agencies.
Are you better than those twenty-six others?

                    MATCHBOX
Paul said you had a type. You favor a certain girl.

                    SUNNY JACK
Can you confirm that by looking at the faces?

                    MATCHBOX
I can. They're all young girls with a figure.

                    SUNNY JACK
I need more than that.

                    MATCHBOX
I can sing. I can dance.

                    SUNNY JACK
Can you act?

                    MATCHBOX
Absolutely.

                    SUNNY JACK
You had any training?

                    MATCHBOX
At an academy?

                    SUNNY JACK
Yeah, any kind of lessons.

                    MATCHBOX
Back in Ohio, I had--

                    SUNNY JACK
Tap classes. Ballet. Little girl in a tutu.

                    MATCHBOX
I outgrew my tutu years ago.

                              SUNNY JACK thinks. He takes out a
                              cigarette and a large box of
                              matches from his jacket pocket.
                              He taps the cigarette on the box,
                              never taking his eyes from the
                              girl.

                    MATCHBOX (Continued)
If you want I can... sing for you, or do a monologue.
This is an audition, right?

                    SUNNY JACK
I like to know a girl first. I like a little
foreplay.

                    MATCHBOX
Are you looking for a special audition? This is a
motel room.

                    SUNNY JACK
I told you, I don't make dirty pictures.

                    MATCHBOX
Casting couch. Isn't that what they call it?

                    SUNNY JACK
No. That's not me.

                         Pause.

                    MATCHBOX
So you want a monologue then, or is this still
foreplay?

                    SUNNY JACK
Okay. Mah-no-log. From what?

                    MATCHBOX
You like Williams?

                    SUNNY JACK
You a Stella or a Blanche?

                    MATCHBOX
Ste—

                    SUNNY JACK
          (Overlapping)
Stella, of course.

                    He sits back, again staring at
                    her. She smiles, stands, poses,
                    as if that's what he wants to
                    consider.

                    He lights his cigarette and waves
                    her back down into her chair.

                    SUNNY JACK (Continued)
Do you smoke?

                    MATCHBOX
Yes. I smoke.

                    SUNNY JACK
Have one.

                    He does not offer her one of his.

                    Getting wise to the signal, she
                    reaches into her purse, withdraws
                    a pack, and, excruciatingly slow,
                    pulls the tip of a cigarette until
                    it's out of the pack. She pouts

her lips, lightly puts the
cigarette between them, slides the
pack away, and leans forward.

MATCHBOX
Got a light?

Pleased, he holds out his box of
matches.

SUNNY JACK
Keep the box. Two left.

She reaches in, strikes one, never
dropping her cool façade.

MATCHBOX
Never before seen a man carry a whole box of matches
around. Most people carry packs. You a pyromaniac?

He laughs.

SUNNY JACK
You never know when you're going to need a whole
shitload of matches.

MATCHBOX takes the box from him,
with its one last match rattling,
and tucks it in her handbag.

SUNNY JACK (Continued)
Forget your name. I'm going to call you Matchbox.

MATCHBOX
That wouldn't look very good on a marquee.

                    SUNNY JACK
It's a trick I have. Name the girls you like with
something weird. These days, names all blend into a
pile of mush. Janes and Jennifers. That's why the
world invented nicknames, you know? To keep us better
separated. Right, Match... Box? See: rolls off
tongue.

                    MATCHBOX
Okay. If I have one for you. I'll call you... Sunny
Jack. For that tan. And that sunshine smile.

                    SUNNY JACK
I do have a good smile. No one's ever named me back.

                              SUNNY JACK circles her in her
                              chair. She remains unfazed.

                    SUNNY JACK (Continued)
Any other desperate dolls down there in that lobby?

                    MATCHBOX
Twenty-six you said.

                    SUNNY JACK
Any of them you dig?

                    MATCHBOX
Depends on your definition.

                    SUNNY JACK
I'm talking about who you might have some chemistry
with on screen. You talk to any of them? Or is
everyone milling around like cats?

                    MATCHBOX
I talked to two girls. I liked them quite a bit.

                    SUNNY JACK
They new to town, too?

                    MATCHBOX
One is from Seattle. Like being off a boat, I
suppose, right, Sunny Jack?

SUNNY JACK

Do me a favor, Matchbox. Go down. Get them. Tell them I want to audition all three of you at the same time. Then tell the rest to beat it, go home.

Blackout.

ACT I

SCENE 5

SOUND: Another retro bubblegum pop
song, distorted, loud, then
fading.

Dim lights rise on the bed where
THE VIL lies, covered up to her
eyes.

The mirror above is now changed,
more like a funhouse mirror than a
clear reflection. She looks at
her body, transfixed. Without
removing the sheet, she raises and
lowers her legs, then turns her
face from side to side.

At last, she sits bolt upright and
SCREAMS at her reflection, then
says:

                    THE VIL
          (Spiteful)
One room is quite like another!

                    The room's door opens slowly by
                    itself. THE VIL turns.

                    After a pause, in walks a man
                    wearing a strange costume party
                    mask, a suit and a necktie draped
                    in clear plastic.

                    THE VIL turns her head slowly and
                    looks at the man. This man is
                    known as: CAPTAIN.

                    THE VIL (Continued)
Don't come any closer. I know who you are now, and,
                    (MORE)

16

THE VIL (Continued)

and, and I'm sorry. I told you, I'm sorry. I want to
go home. I'm sorry. I'll go home, and I won't say
anything to anyone.

CAPTAIN crosses to the filing
cabinet on the other side of the
room. He pulls out three
photographs – the actor headshots
of THE VIL, MATCHBOX, and PRETTY
SEXY. He returns with them to the
bed and lies down beside THE VIL.
She is terrified.

He looks at MATCHBOX's picture,
shows it to her, holds it up to
the mirror so it distorts. He
does the same with PRETTY SEXY.

At last, he inspects THE VIL's
headshot – smiling, perfect. He
holds it up to the funhouse mirror
and looks straight at the real
girl.

Lights fade to blackout.

ACT I

SCENE 6

SOUND: A film projector with la-
la-la music.

A flash of a photograph hits the
corner of the motel room. Another
flash elsewhere. This repeats,
turning the motel room into a
mini-theatre of quickly revolving
still photographs.

The images are of the three girls
-- The Vil, Matchbox, and Pretty
Sexy -- in bright sunlight, happy
together, playing parts in what
appears to be a beach movie.

Beautiful. Happy. Scantily
dressed.

When the flashes stop:

A blare of lights erupts on PRETTY
SEXY as she stands downstage.

SOUND: Light street traffic.

She speaks to someone unseen.

                    PRETTY SEXY
Is it always so bright in this fucking town? I'm
going to go through a whole pile of sunglasses, I can
tell. I buy cheap ones, 'cos I lose them. Where I'm
from, it rains all the time. Of course I'm an
actress! This is Hollywood, isn't it? No, nothing
yet. But soon. Fingers... crossed. Do you have a
stick of gum? No. Okay. What did you say your name
was again? Paul. Gotcha. And what's that other
guy's name again? Jack Fennigan. No, no I haven't.
What kind of pictures? Girl pictures. Ah. Things
                    (MORE)

PRETTY SEXY (Continued)

where girls get- Oh, okay, good. I'm not quite ready
to show my boobs on camera. Not just yet. My
grandmother's still alive. Yes, when she's dead the
world can see my chest. Ha ha. Yes, people have
called me sexy before. Right before they tried to
touch my leg under the dinner table. So I'm used to
it, yes. But I got talent. Yes, Paul, I am pretty
sexy. I know, I know. Remind me not to go to dinner
with you any time soon. You'd be all over me like a
cheap wig. Uh huh. Yeah. Uh huh. One o'clock
today? Uh huh. Okay. No plans. Why a motel? Oh,
that's common? Okay. What should I wear? I mean,
what's the part? What will impress this Jack F.? Be
myself. Pretty. Sexy. Gotcha. Thanks for the card.
Yes, I'll be there. I know. I'll be there. But if
it's squirrelly, I'm leaving. I'm a good girl. Don't
want involved in that stuff. Okay, Paul. Okay.

Lights fade.

ACT I

SCENE 7

Rise on the motel room, sun
through the window.

THE VIL is dressed in a bikini and
sits on the edge of the bed. She
sighs a big, bored sigh.

She stands and approaches the
cabinet. She flips through files,
reads.

SOUND: The telephone rings.

She quickly puts away the
materials and answers the call.

                    THE VIL
Jack Fennigan Productions.

                    SUNNY JACK
          (Over telephone)
Hey, doll.

                    THE VIL
Oh, hey!

                    SUNNY JACK
So severe.

                    THE VIL
Well, I just thought I better sound official.

                    SUNNY JACK
Are you wearing it?

                    THE VIL
Yes, I'm wearing it.

                    SUNNY JACK
Fits?

                        THE VIL
Of course it fits.   Jack, you know this body well.

                        SUNNY JACK
Look, I'm tied up.   I'm gonna need a few more hours.

                        THE VIL
But the sun will be starting to go down.

                        SUNNY JACK
I'm make it up to you.

                        THE VIL
No, I'm *going*.   I said I wanted to go to the beach and
I'm going...

                        SUNNY JACK
Call the Mouseketeers.

                        THE VIL
Yeah, I could call them, I guess.   Okay.   I will.   So
I'll see you tonight?

                        SUNNY JACK
Don't wash it off.

                        THE VIL
Yes, baby, I'll smell like *sand*.   I know you love it.
'Bye, Jack.   Don't work too hard.

                        SUNNY JACK
See ya, doll.

                        She hangs up.

                        She dials another number.

                        SOUND: Rings through telephone, an
                        answer.

                        MATCHBOX
                 (Over telephone)
Hello?

                          THE VIL
It's me. I've been waiting the whole time. Jack
stood me up for some meeting at the lot. Want to come
and distract silly boys on surfboards until they
drown?

                          MATCHBOX
Should I call our favorite (blonde/redhead/brunette)?

                          THE VIL
If you don't mind the competition.

                          MATCHBOX
Maybe I'm hers -- you ever think of that?

                          THE VIL
I'll meet you at the usual.
          (Conspiratorially)
Jack bought me a new bikini.

                          MATCHBOX
Of *course* he did. Kisses!

                              THE VIL hangs up. She starts to
                              pack a bag for the beach. She
                              starts to put on a skirt.

                              As she does, the door comes open!

                              Standing there is CAPTAIN. He
                              wears no mask this time, but still
                              has plastic over his suit and tie.
                              He holds a toolbox in one hand, a
                              room key in the other. He has a
                              slightly regal disposition, even
                              in these circumstances.

                              Startled, THE VIL gives a short
                              yelp and yanks up her skirt.

                          CAPTAIN
Mr. Fennigan told me before he left that I could come
and inspect your shower.

22

                    THE VIL
Oh. Are you with the motel?

                    CAPTAIN
People call me Captain.

                    THE VIL
Captain? You the owner then?

                    CAPTAIN
I just... fix things that are broken.

                    THE VIL
Okay. Well, come on in. I'm leaving in a sec. I
just have a few more things to get together.

                         CAPTAIN enters. He goes to the
                         bathroom and sets down his
                         toolbox.

                         THE VIL, back turned to him, rubs
                         on aerosol antiperspirant.

                    THE VIL (Continued)
What's with the plastic?

                    CAPTAIN
So I don't get wet. I hate being wet. What about
you? You hate being wet?

                    THE VIL
No, I'm wet a lot. This town's too hot.

                         CAPTAIN takes out a radio from
                         inside his toolbox. He places it
                         on the cabinet and turns it on.

                         SOUND: Retro bubblegum pop emits
                         from the radio.

                    CAPTAIN
I like music.

                        THE VIL
No problem. It doesn't bother me.

                        CAPTAIN
You been in L.A. long?

                        THE VIL
Ah, just about three months. Longer than some.
Longer than my friends. I'm an actress.

                        CAPTAIN
Mr. Fennigan makes movies. He told me. Cheapies.

                        THE VIL
Cheapies? He's not Louie B. Mayer, if that's what you
mean. I was in *Girls from Venice Beach*. Did you see
that? No. I figured. I played the bad girl. I was
the villain. That's how I got my nickname. My
friends call me The Vil. Or Vil, for short. I need
to get my beach towel. Excuse me.

                        CAPTAIN flattens against the wall
                        and she slides past and reaches to
                        pull a towel from the unseen rack.
                        As she does so, CAPTAIN tugs her
                        bikini string and her top unties.
                        She catches the bikini top just
                        before it falls.

                        THE VIL (Continued)
What are you doing?

                        Still holding her top, she grabs
                        her towel.

                        THE VIL (Continued)
Better be a goddamn accident.

                        CAPTAIN
            (Urgently)
I'm a friend.

                    THE VIL
Move.

                              She turns to leave the bathroom,
                              but he blocks her, stays in close.

                              CAPTAIN holds her in place.

                    CAPTAIN
I wanted to meet you, but Jack wouldn't let me.

                    THE VIL
I will hit you so hard that you will shit your plastic
pants.

                    CAPTAIN
I'm not with the motel. I can help you.

                              CAPTAIN lays his hand on her hand
                              that holds the bikini.

                              SOUND: The radio changes,
                              distorts, becomes an alien sound.
                              Now, CAPTAIN's voice comes out of
                              it.

                    CAPTAIN
          (Over radio)
I want you to listen to what I say. I want you do
what I tell you. I'm not wearing this because I'm
afraid of water.

                    THE VIL
You're not afraid.

                              CAPTAIN moves his hand down and
                              her hand comes with his, revealing
                              her skin beneath.

                    CAPTAIN
          (Over radio)
I'm not what you think I am. You are right to be
scared of me. You think you're a villain?

                                                            25

                    THE VIL
You're the villain.

                    CAPTAIN
That's right... It's me!

                    SOUND: Radio turns to blindingly
                    loud static.

                    Blackout.

ACT I

SCENE 8

Strobes.

SOUND: Busy signal from a telephone throughout...

The "movie" from before plays, only now, it's a bit more disturbing. The photos flashed are not of three girls in the sun, but of a darker, more violent texture. A forest. Shadowed. Lost.

The movie stops suddenly, but the telephone continues on.

PRETTY SEXY comes out of the bathroom and looks down at the buzzing motel telephone.

She is hesitant but, at last, she picks it up and puts it back in its cradle. After a moment, she picks it up again.

SOUND: Retro bubblegum pop plays over the telephone.

Confused, she hangs up.

Enter SUNNY JACK, who is startled to see PRETTY SEXY in the room.

                    SUNNY JACK
Why hello.

                    PRETTY SEXY
Hi ya, Jack.

                    SUNNY JACK
What brings you to my neck of the woods?

                    PRETTY SEXY
Let's be honest, Jack. This isn't your woods at all.

                    SUNNY JACK
What are you talking about?

                    PRETTY SEXY
Paul's got loose lips.

                    SUNNY JACK
Oh, really. That was almost your nickname.

                    PRETTY SEXY
Dirty boy.

                    SUNNY JACK
And that was almost mine.
          (Resigned)
So what did Paul tell you? He tell you about Bel
Aire?

                    PRETTY SEXY
Bel Aire and a girl named Claudette. From your French
excursion. Thinking of making *Girls from Riviera
Beach* now, Jack, or did you just tell her that to get
her on a jet to Hollywood? She could be the kind of
girl you like.

                    SUNNY JACK
You don't know what I like. Not at all.

                    PRETTY SEXY
Maybe you're right, maybe you're right. I'm a dummy.
But The Vil isn't. Technically, she was my friend
before you were. Only by, say, an hour in a motel
lobby, but an hour's an hour.

                    SUNNY JACK
I'm not knifing Vil. She's my girl. Claudette's just
an actress I met and liked. She's in town on her own
motor and I gave her somewhere to stay until she finds
a place.

PRETTY SEXY

You know, it's weird, Jack, that you have permanent residence in this crap motel when you have a nice place for a nice girl in Bel Aire. How come The Vil doesn't get the sweet accommodations? She gets the dirty mattress.

SUNNY JACK

You're funny.

> JACK takes PRETTY SEXY by the shoulders and guides her, somewhat against her will, to sit on the mattress. He lays her flat. He lays beside her. They both look up at the mirror.

SUNNY JACK (Continued)

The mattress is just fine.

PRETTY SEXY

Makes for nice casting, doesn't it, Jack?

SUNNY JACK

You tell me.
(Points to mirror)
What do you see there, Sexy? You know what I see? I see a beautiful woman. I see a woman with some talent. Probably a little older than she's sayin', but that's okay. We're all older than we're saying. She escapes from rainy, *depressing* Seattle, where, perhaps, there was some trouble. And, out of a sudden inspiration, she decides: it's now or never. And it was *me* who found you! Via Paul, of course, my trusty field agent. After a *long* audition -- yes -- a few hours of jokes and a dinner, the four of us find ourselves back here. You get the part. Two pictures. In the second, you got to rob banks and you liked it.
(Pause)
You're not as dangerous in real life as you were on that screen. But you're pretty sexy in both.

PRETTY SEXY

I'll tell you what I see. Here lies a man who likes women. Young ones. He likes them so much he makes
(MORE)

29

                    PRETTY SEXY (Continued)
movies just to have them in his company. And, one
day, he thinks he'll discover a star. And that star
is *not* me. It's Vil. So you keep her close. Not
because you're jealous, but because she may be worth a
lot of money one day.

                    SUNNY JACK
Is that what you think? I'm grooming her for the red
carpet?

                    PRETTY SEXY
        (Thrown)
Well. Sure. Why not? You have to have some reason
for keeping her so tight under your arm.

                    SUNNY JACK
Matchbox is the only one of you three that can act.

                         PRETTY SEXY sits up, something in
                         her face. Then re-engages.

                    PRETTY SEXY
But can she do this?

                         PRETTY SEXY undoes SUNNY JACK's
                         belt. She curls up near to him.

                    SUNNY JACK
You think I'm going around Vil's back? Look at you.

                    PRETTY SEXY
Maybe I'm just showing off how good I am with belts.
Want to see how good I am with buttons?

                         PRETTY SEXY slowly pops the top
                         button on her sweater. Then the
                         next, then the next, then the
                         next. She opens her blouse and
                         reveals the bra beneath.

SUNNY JACK
What about your grandma?

PRETTY SEXY
What about your girlfriend?

SUNNY JACK
Last time you and me were like this, Vil wasn't my
girlfriend. She was my audition. And think about it.
Maybe not then, but maybe it's in your mind now. I'm
old enough to be your father.

PRETTY SEXY
Or my boyfriend. I like older men. What to see how I
am with zippers?

She unzips his pants.

PRETTY SEXY (Continued)
Where is she?

SUNNY JACK
I don't know. She disappears sometimes.

PRETTY SEXY
Will she be coming home in the next hour?

SUNNY JACK
And if she does?

PRETTY SEXY
Lock the door.

SUNNY JACK
She has a key.

PRETTY SEXY
Does it really matter if she finds you with me or with
the French slut?

SUNNY JACK
You heard about Claudette so you thought I'd go for
you, too. You want to be a star?

31

                    PRETTY SEXY
I want to be a star.

                         He quickly, roughly pins her to
                         the bed.

                    SUNNY JACK
Tell me you want it! Men sleep with women because
they want it. Women sleep with men because they want
something. Tell me. Make me believe it!

                    PRETTY SEXY
I want to be a star.

                    SUNNY JACK
Say it again!

                    PRETTY SEXY
I want to be a star!

                         She worms her legs around him. He
                         pins her, but doesn't go in for
                         her yet. She writhes.

                         They kiss.

                         SOUND: The telephone rings.

                         They don't stop.

                         After a moment, SUNNY JACK breaks
                         away. He goes to the ringing
                         telephone.

                         PRETTY SEXY undresses beneath the
                         sheets.

                         SUNNY JACK picks up the phone.

                         SOUND: Retro bubblegum over the
                         receiver.

                    SUNNY JACK
Hello?

He slowly hangs up.

She's waiting.

He drifts... then dives into bed.

Blackout.

ACT I

SCENE 9

SOUND: Running water.

THE VIL sits on the end of the
bed, doll-like, in the dim motel
room.

SUNNY JACK enters.

                    SUNNY JACK
You're back.

He crosses, puts his stuff down
then hears the running water. He
investigates.

                    SUNNY JACK (Continued)
How long's the water been on? You taking a shower?

She doesn't respond.

He goes inside the bathroom and
shuts off the water.

Back in the room, he leans against
the wall and crosses his arms.

                    SUNNY JACK (Continued)
Where you been?
          (No answer)
Didn't used to be like this. First few months. I
could count on you.
          (Pause)
You got another guy?
          (No answer)
What's wrong?
          (No answer)
You can go, you know. Not like we're married. Do
people even get married anymore? This town. What's
the point? Vil? Are you listening?

                         THE VIL
I think something's wrong with me. I'm not myself
when I'm away from you. But some things don't change.
Does every motel in L.A. look like this one?

                       SUNNY JACK
Is that what you do -- go to other motels? Hell,
doll, if you need a change of scenery, I can—

                         THE VIL
When are we going to make another movie, Jack?

                       SUNNY JACK
I'm working on it. Paul wants to direct. I'm close
on the money.

                         THE VIL
Who do I play this time? I want to be someone
different than me.

                       SUNNY JACK
No script yet. I... wasn't sure if you were coming
back. There are a few girls in line so far. French
girl. And Pretty Sexy wants a piece. Might be
something for you if you stick long enough.

                         THE VIL
Jack... why didn't you take me to the beach that day?

                       SUNNY JACK
What?

                         THE VIL
Last summer. Why didn't you take me to the beach?

                       SUNNY JACK
Jesus, that was months ago.

                         THE VIL
If you had come home on time and we went to the beach.
Oh, God. I'm so scared all the time.

                  SUNNY JACK sits with her.

                    SUNNY JACK
Listen. You need what I call "movie therapy." Let's
go see a few flicks. Something old. Something stupid
and light. A musical.

                    THE VIL
Matchbox is dead.

                    SUNNY JACK
Is that a joke?

                    THE VIL
She's dead. Last night. She was found in her
apartment on La Cienega. Someone cut her up in the
shower and then reassembled her on the bed using
stitches you'd find in a rag doll.

                    SUNNY JACK
That's terrible. These things don't make the papers?
How'd you hear?

                    THE VIL
I found her.

                    She breaks down, holds him.

                    THE VIL (Continued)
Jack, Jack. Sometimes, I don't know who I am. I
can't remember things. I can't remember you. I don't
know where I live. It scares me. I go to a motel and
walk up the stairs and into the room and it's not this
room, it's someone else's, and they come home and say,
"How did you get in here?" And I can't explain,
because my key worked. It worked. But I can't
remember opening the door. Something is happening to
me, Jack.

                    SUNNY JACK
Vil, calm down. You're fine. Doll, you're fine.
All this - this is about Matchbox. What you saw. Did
you go to the police? We'll go to the police. I'll
take you right now.

                    She shakes her head, buries herself in
                    him.

SUNNY JACK (Continued)
You'll get better, you will. You'll stay here. With
me. I won't let you leave my side. You'll never
disappear again.

THE VIL
I don't want to leave you.

SUNNY JACK
Stay. I love you. Stay.

She pulls away.

SUNNY JACK (Continued)
Don't look surprised. Of course I love you. You're
my star. You know, I've had a lot of girlfriends,
it's true. But I've never told any that I loved them.

THE VIL
I'm your star.

SUNNY JACK
The brightest. I'm holding onto you until I burn.

Lights fade.

ACT I

SCENE 10

SOUND: Mechanics.

Strobes.

CAPTAIN, in mask, enters, walking stiffly, slowly. He heads for the cabinet.

MATCHBOX can be seen just behind the bedpost, but only her eyes and the top of her head.

CAPTAIN opens the cabinet, takes out files, and spills them on the floor. He picks up photographs of actresses and places them on the bed.

MATCHBOX's eyes watch as CAPTAIN rips the photos up on the bed and then begins to lean into them, sexually.

MATCHBOX comes around from the bed, screaming, only there is no sound except for the roaring mechanics.

CAPTAIN sees MATCHBOX for the first time. As she screams, CAPTAIN leaves the bed, enters the bathroom then locates his toolbox and returns. He throws MATCHBOX on the bed and begins to tear at her the way he tore at the photographs.

Just as she begins to come apart...

Blackout.

ACT I

SCENE 11

Lights rise.

SUNNY JACK, alone in the motel.

<u>SOUND</u>: The telephone rings.

He picks it up on first chime, as
if waiting for it.

SUNNY JACK
Yes, I'm here. Come on up. Third floor. You'll have
to walk, I'm afraid. Okay, then.

He hangs up the telephone.

Lights fade.

ACT I

SCENE 12

Lights rise.

MATCHBOX is again behind the bedpost.

THE VIL sits on the mattress.

PRETTY SEXY is in the bathroom with her back turned.

SOUND: Dull voices from other rooms.

             THE VIL
This isn't my motel.

             PRETTY SEXY
        (Offstage)
No. It's mine.

PRETTY SEXY turns; she's putting on makeup.

             PRETTY SEXY (Continued)
She comes to see me, too, you know.

             THE VIL
Is she here now?

             PRETTY SEXY
I don't see her.

THE VIL rises and inspects behind the bed. Even though MATCHBOX actually *is* there, she's apparently invisible.

THE VIL
No. No, I don't see her either.

PRETTY SEXY
Maybe she's hiding from you. When she comes out, she
scares the bejesus out of me. Never believed in
ghosts. Never believed in much besides movies. You
know, I met an agent. Jack introduced us and we hit
it off. He's a strange pet. But I hear he's
connected. He tells me he's seen our stuff and he
liked what I did. He's coming to the set next week.
What can I do to sabotage the French flower?

THE VIL
Just do your best performance.

                    PRETTY SEXY exits the bathroom,
                    moves to the closet.

PRETTY SEXY
I show my boobs in this one. Didn't take as much
convincing as I thought.

THE VIL
I want to act again.

PRETTY SEXY
Then do it.

THE VIL
Most days I, I don't even know where I am. How can I
act? How can I act it? Pretend. Make movies with
scenes out of order. Big, black holes where things
are supposed to have happened. Important things.
Thing I should know. Things I should remember.

PRETTY SEXY
Okay, weirdo.

                    THE VIL tries to smile.

                    Long pause.

                    THE VIL
Have you ever been hypnotized?

                         PRETTY SEXY registers something.

                         PRETTY SEXY
What an oddball question.

                    THE VIL
Have you? Have you?

                    PRETTY SEXY
Why do you care?

                    THE VIL
I want to know.

                         PRETTY SEXY considers before
                         answering.

                    PRETTY SEXY
Well, well. Okay. I saw this one show in Seattle.
At a club. I was pulled up by this old man who said
he could put me in a spell of suggestion and the
audience would give me a command later in the show.
He goes through his whole bit with a pocket watch and
then, at the last second, he leans into my ear and
whispers, "We're going to have some fun with them
tonight and, if you play along, there's a hundred
dollars in it for you." I'm an actress, right? He
must have seen it. Knew that I'd perform the hell out
of it. So I pretend to be under his spell and he gets
the command from the audience. Most in the crowd are
men who want me to take off my bra and wave it in the
air when the old man says the word, "Shocking!" I
wasn't very comfortable with the idea of waving my
bra, but I liked the idea of a hundred dollars for so
little effort. Twenty minutes later in the show, he
says "shocking," but I wasn't paying any attention.
He kind of gives me a harsh look and repeats the word.
Like a zombie, I stand up, unhook my bra, ease it down
                         (MORE)

PRETTY SEXY (Continued)

off my shoulders, and wave it like it was the American flag. The men cheer, he wakes me up, and I sit down, like nothing at all happened. Except that you can see through my shirt. At the end of the show, a woman meets me at the door. She asks me to follow her backstage. She says the old magician needs to "un-hypnotize me," so at every mention of the word "shocking" from that night forward won't affect me. I suppose she doesn't know about the hundred bucks, but this must be the magician's ruse to get me my payday. So, backstage... everyone's gone and I'm waiting for the old man. After what seems like forever, he comes in behind the curtain and I snap, "Where's my hundred dollars?" And he... claps... twice, like this, very fast.

(Pause)

Midnight, I wake up in a motel room... a room much like this one. I'm in a chair. My clothes are on, but buttoned wrong. My panties are missing. There's a hundred dollar bill on the bed. And I'm alone.

THE VIL

Oh my God.

PRETTY SEXY

A little while later, I got real sore between my legs, and I got a very bad yeast infection that took a month to cure.

THE VIL

Did you tell the police?

PRETTY SEXY

The motel room was registered in my name and paid for by me. I had no evidence anything had happened. But I'm pretty certain I was raped.

PRETTY SEXY stops. Looks to THE VIL. Shakes it off.

PRETTY SEXY (Continued)

So what makes you ask about hypnosis?

43

The light in the bathroom begins
to grow brighter and brighter.

SOUND: A growing electrical hum,
matching the light.

PRETTY SEXY (Continued)

She's here.

Lights fade to blackout as
MATCHBOX lifts from behind the
bed.

ACT I

SCENE 13

Dim lights rise.

MATCHBOX, as at the start of Act
I, lays on the bed, alone, looking
at the mirror.

                    MATCHBOX
Look at you. You pathetic bitch. Look at you.

She opens then closes her legs.

                    MATCHBOX (Continued)
You'd like that. Wouldn't you? Look at you. You're
as bad as the rest.

SOUND: A knock on the door.

MATCHBOX covers her exposed body
with the white sheet.

                    MATCHBOX (Continued)
Come...

The door opens by itself. No one
enters.

After a pause, MATCHBOX sits up,
holding the sheet in place.

                    MATCHBOX (Continued)
Is that you? Captain? Is that you?

She rises, wraps the sheet around
her shoulders, goes to the door,
and slowly shuts it.

SOUND: Another knock.

MATCHBOX (Continued)
(To door, in whisper)
Is that you?

SUNNY JACK
(Through door)
It's Jack.

MATCHBOX
How did you know where to find me?

SUNNY JACK
(Through door)
Vil told me. Can I come in?

MATCHBOX starts to dress.

MATCHBOX
Just a moment.

At last, she opens. SUNNY JACK
stands at the door. She pauses
then gestures for him to enter.

SUNNY JACK
Did you meet him?

MATCHBOX
(Weighing words, a bit weary)
I did.

SUNNY JACK
Did you like him?

MATCHBOX
Oh... I've been thinking about him a lot.

SUNNY JACK
Did he like you?

                    MATCHBOX
He did.

                    SUNNY JACK
Then why didn't you come and talk to me? Did he offer
you a contract?

                    MATCHBOX
Yes. He says that I will live forever.

                    SUNNY JACK
I suppose congratulations are in order. *Annie Get
Your Gun*, two of my flicks, and you're off to bigger
and better.

                    MATCHBOX
How come you didn't introduce him to the other girls?

                    SUNNY JACK
Oh, I dunno... Sexy might get her shot. She's willing
to do a lot to move up. Vil is my girl. I want to
make sure the circumstances are right for her.

                    MATCHBOX
You never thanked me. For introducing you two. I was
the one who held her hand in that... what do you call
it? Audition.

                    SUNNY JACK
It *was* an audition.

                    MATCHBOX
You have a peculiar style of such.

                    SUNNY JACK
What do you care, you got the part? And now look at
you. I'll bet you'll be on *The Mod Squad* before then
end of the summer.

                    MATCHBOX
Did your last "finds" go on to such legitimate
heights?

                    SUNNY JACK smiles and thinks.

                         SUNNY JACK
Well. You're in good hands now. Better hands. I
just wanted to make sure you were all right. I didn't
hear from you since the introduction. So I assumed it
went bad and you were pouting. You're too talented to
pout. Next time pick up a telephone.

                    He crosses to exit.

                         MATCHBOX
Sunny Jack?

                    He stops.

                         MATCHBOX (Continued)
Got any matches?

                    He holds then wrestles out a box
                    and tosses it on the bed.

                         SUNNY JACK
Keep 'em. Good luck, Matchbox. I always liked you.

                    He exits.

                    MATCHBOX lights a cigarette.

                    Lights fade.

ACT I

SCENE 14

Lights rise on the empty motel room.

SOUND: Bubblegum pop music.

From the bathroom, CAPTAIN enters, wearing mask. He centers and stands before the audience, a mystery behind his mask.

Strobes.

SOUND: The projector runs. The music and the mechanics compete for dominance.

A movie begins, flashes and pictures, this time more violent than ever, with nudity, a psychotic fugue.

THE VIL enters into the cacophony.

She covers her ears and screams at intervals, staggering around the motel room, tearing at it, taking out the files from the cabinet, taking pillows and sheets off the bed.

All the while: CAPTAIN stares at the audience and does not break.

Crescendo.

Sudden stop to blackout.

Curtain.

ACT II

SCENE 1

Lights rise on the motel room.

It is cleared of the destruction
from the previous Act I. However,
the mattress remains bare, without
bed sheets.

A key is heard in the door and
SUNNY JACK enters. He walks in a
daze. He sits on the bed, strokes
the mattress, and becomes teary-
eyed.

                    SUNNY JACK
I'm sorry. I couldn't do anything. I tried to save
you, doll. If you're anywhere but heaven or hell,
know that I, I love you. I'm trying to reach you. I
love you. I love you.

He thinks he hears something. At
last, quickly, he exits.

Long pause.

Slowly, THE VIL crawls out from
under the bed as...

SOUND: Low beats and hissing.

She goes to the motel room door.

She pulls the knob, tries to get
it open. She bangs on the door.

She backs up, turns to the
audience, and for the first time
we see that her face is covered in
stitches.

She continues scratching at the
door, animalistic.

Lights and sounds fade.

ACT II

SCENE 2

Lights rise on the motel room.

PRETTY SEXY stands alone, flipping through photographs.

SOUND: The telephone rings.

She doesn't answer.

                SUNNY JACK
        (From offstage)
You going to get that?

        The ringing stops.

        She continues inspecting
        photographs.

        SUNNY JACK steps out of the
        bathroom, wiping his hands on a
        towel...

                SUNNY JACK (Continued)
You didn't answer?

                PRETTY SEXY
You don't live here anymore. We shouldn't be
answering the telephone.
        (Indicating photographs)
Why do you keep all these?

                SUNNY JACK
You never know when someone will come walking back
through my door. Also, I want proof of age. Un-
agented girls must be eighteen or older to audition.

        Lazily, she discards the
        photographs.

                    PRETTY SEXY
Can you do hypnosis?

                    SUNNY JACK
Hypnosis? Hell no.

                    PRETTY SEXY
Do you know any hypnotists?

                    SUNNY JACK
Nope.
          (Gestures to photographs)
What did the cards tell you?

                    PRETTY SEXY
No, sorry. Hypnosis wasn't listed as any special
skills. Lots of dancing and singing. Pity you never
did a Broadway show. One girl claims can stand still
for long periods of time. Not sure if that's a skill,
though, or just creepy.

                    SUNNY JACK
I don't know. Could be a skill. Depends on what kind
of movie you're making. Is that why you wanted me to
come back here? To look at old shots and find
yourself a hypnotist. I think there's an easier way.
L.A. Times has dollar advertisements for just that
kind of kook.

                    PRETTY SEXY
Last time I saw Vil, she said she thought she had been
hypnotized.

                    SUNNY JACK
Did she now.

                    PRETTY SEXY wanders, saying
                    nothing.

                    SUNNY JACK (Continued)
Do you believe in that? I don't. I believe in drugs.
                    (MORE)

                    SUNNY JACK (Continued)
I bet a person can be drugged into believing
something, anything. People are schmucks. Why do you
think there's a rocketship effects department? Fool
people into thinking there are Martians. But
mesmerism - I always thought that was a crock.

                    PRETTY SEXY
          (Shrugs)
It's what she told me.

                    SUNNY JACK
          (Doubtful)
Vil... was hypnotized?

                    PRETTY SEXY
A few weeks before she died, she told me she suspected
that she had been hypnotized.

                    SUNNY JACK
How could she be hypnotized without her permission?

                    PRETTY SEXY
She didn't know *how* it happened. But... she thought
she knew *when* it happened. She told me you and her
had made some plans to go to the beach. On that day,
you telephoned and said you would be late. That's the
last thing in her head. She never met with me and I
thought she was flaky. I teased her later. But after
that... lost day... she started blacking out. She'd
be in the middle of a thing, lose track, then hours
later, or days later, wake in a strange motels across
Hollywood with no idea how she got there or whom she
had been with.

                    SUNNY JACK
She slept with other men?

                    PRETTY SEXY
I asked her that. She couldn't remember. She did
feel, though, that she had done something awful. I'm
sorry. I'm sorry I have to tell you that. Do you
know what else she said? That Matchbox came to visit
her... as a ghost.

                    SOUND: The telephone rings.

                    SUNNY JACK looks to her. She
                    doesn't move. At last, he
                    answers.

                    SOUND: Retro bubblegum over the
                    telephone.

                    SUNNY JACK pulls the telephone
                    from his ear and turns to PRETTY
                    SEXY.

                    SUNNY JACK
Come here.

                    PRETTY SEXY
Who is it? No one knows we're here.

                    He holds out the telephone and she
                    listens, takes it.

                    SUNNY JACK
This has happened before on this phone. I thought it
was a crossed wire.

                    Saying nothing, she hangs up.

                    SUNNY JACK (Continued)
Some kind of joke.

                    PRETTY SEXY picks up her purse and
                    goes into the bathroom, out of
                    sight.

                    He drifts back to the telephone,
                    considering.

                    SUNNY JACK (Continued)
I mean, don't you think that's odd? That tune, over
and over on this line?

The bathroom door shuts.

Pause.

Jack sits at the desk.

SOUND: The telephone rings again.

SUNNY JACK picks it up on first
chime, as if waiting for it.
(This is a repeat of Act I: Scene
11's start.)

                    SUNNY JACK (Continued)
Yes, I'm here. Come on up. Third floor. You'll have
to walk, I'm afraid. Okay, then.

There is a sudden knock on the
motel room door and SUNNY JACK
answers it. CAPTAIN, without mask
and with briefcase rather than
toolbox, stands expectant.

                    SUNNY JACK (Continued)
What did you do, fly?

No answer.

                    SUNNY JACK (Continued)
You just called.

                    CAPTAIN
I was in the lobby.

                    SUNNY JACK
I know. But. Jesus, okay, come in.

CAPTAIN enters, looks around the
room.

                    SUNNY JACK (Continued)
Have a seat. Here, I'll get you a chair.

                    He unfolds one of the chairs
                    against the wall and, satisfied,
                    gestures.

                    SUNNY JACK (Continued)
Sorry. Not luxury, I know, but you should have seen
my last office. And they say there're no basements in
L.A. Place was a cavern. Safe in an earthquake,
though, if we ever get the big one. I still have the
lease for just that possibility.

                    CAPTAIN sits.

                    CAPTAIN
One motel room is quite like another.

                    SUNNY JACK
I suppose you're right.

                    CAPTAIN
Are we alone?

                    SUNNY JACK
Sure.

                    CAPTAIN
I like doing business in confidence.

                    SUNNY JACK
So you said.

                    CAPTAIN opens his briefcase, pulls
                    out some papers and inspects them.

                                                        57

                    SUNNY JACK (Continued)
Contracts? So soon. We haven't even started to talk
turkey.

                    CAPTAIN
I come prepared. It steers the conversation.

                    SUNNY JACK
Now I see why they call you Captain.

                    CAPTAIN
I saw your last film, Mr. Fennigan. *Devil House*.

                    SUNNY JACK
Good flick. I can do better.

                    CAPTAIN
I rarely go to the cinema much anymore. I used to see
them all the time, but I got very bored. All of them
were beginning to look the same.

                    SUNNY JACK
I know your type. In the business, but hate the
product.

                    CAPTAIN
I could tell just from the posters that there was a
growing desert in the imagination. But lately, I've
taken in a few shows and it's got my juices flowing.
I particularly like seeing ones when there are very
few people in the theatre. Maybe just one or two.

                    SUNNY JACK
Sounds like *Devil House*, all right. It wasn't a great
smash.

                    CAPTAIN
Oh, but it was. It was to me.

                              CAPTAIN reviews his paperwork. At
                              last, he smiles, sets the papers
                              aside, and pulls a photograph from
                              the case.

                    CAPTAIN (Continued)
Do you know this girl?

                    SUNNY JACK
That's Cindy Valentine.

                    CAPTAIN
Have you seen her movies?

                    SUNNY JACK
One or two. She's good. Where's she been lately?

                    CAPTAIN
She's under contract to me.

            He takes out another photograph.

                    CAPTAIN (Continued)
Do you know her?

                    SUNNY JACK
Amanda LaSalle. She auditioned for me about two years
ago, when she was seventeen.

                    CAPTAIN
But you didn't hire her?

                    SUNNY JACK
No. But now I wish I did. She really blossomed.

                    CAPTAIN
She's under contract to me.

            He takes out another photograph.

                    CAPTAIN (Continued)
How about her?

                    SUNNY JACK
No.

            CAPTAIN glances at the picture.

                    CAPTAIN
You don't recognize her?

                    SUNNY JACK
No. But I don't know every face in town.

                    CAPTAIN
Scarlet Raines.

                    SUNNY JACK takes the picture into
                    his hands, surprised.

                    SUNNY JACK
No shit. She looks young. Wasn't she mur—

                    CAPTAIN snatches back the picture,
                    puts it in the case, and shuts it.

                    CAPTAIN
She would have had a bright future.

                    SUNNY JACK
I agree.

                    CAPTAIN
I think you're going to have a bright future.

                    SUNNY JACK
Are you a fortune-teller?

                    CAPTAIN
I know talent. I like talent. I think you can help
me. Those actresses in *Devil House* were all very...
talented.

                    SUNNY JACK
I'm sorry. I don't understand what kind of
arrangement you're proposing.

                    CAPTAIN
I want you to be my scout.

SUNNY JACK

I have a scout. His name is Paul.

CAPTAIN

Ah, Paul.

SUNNY JACK

Paul tells me you have a lot of sway in this town.
You can get movies made. You know people with money.

CAPTAIN

I do have sway. I'm thankful that Paul has arranged
this meeting so I can... sway.

SUNNY JACK

But I thought you wanted to talk about production
funding. I didn't realize you were after my girls.

CAPTAIN

Your girls? Do you have contracts?

SUNNY JACK

Just per picture. I'm not a studio with central
casting.

CAPTAIN

Don't make it sound so nefarious. Mr. Fennigan. I
can do you a great many favors. You have an eye for
actresses. And your eye is similar to my eye.

SUNNY JACK

Similar eye for recognizing talent?

CAPTAIN

That's what I'm saying.

SUNNY JACK

Uh huh. What if it's is not talent we similarly
recognize?

CAPTAIN

I wouldn't presuppose my tastes in anything.

SUNNY JACK

No, sure. Sure. And I don't mean to imply you're...
what'd you say, nefarious? This town's got a side
that's lies just beyond the disappointments. A
blackness. Horrors that are like deep cuts in the
skin. People you wouldn't want to know in a million
years.

CAPTAIN

Do you not want to know me?

SUNNY JACK

I'm considering.

CAPTAIN stands, picks up his case
and his paperwork.

CAPTAIN

I can't spend my days looking for just the right
girls. I need someone. Someone who wants to be
successful. You help me acquire some talent, I will
make sure they become something more. It's great to
have a name in your picture, right? One of these
actresses could go on to television. That makes the
rights to your little film worth much, much more.
More theaters. More work. A bigger crowd. Imagine
how much money Marilyn Monroe would have made her
early benefactors if she had started in independents?
That's possible now. The era of the smaller picture.
You sign girls to a picture-by-picture deal because
you never know where the money's coming from. But now
you'll know. The good ones will go on. And the
others will stay in your stable of players, acting in
films that can now more readily find funding. Your
scripts. Your choices. Your rewards. I think this
sounds like a very wonderful bargain for you, all in
exchange for just a few introductions. After all, the
girls are not forced into contract with me. It's a
two-way arrangement, Mr. Fennigan. Or should I call
you Mr. DeMille?

SUNNY JACK
            (Smiles)
Now you're just being hurtful.

                    CAPTAIN precisely rests the
                    paperwork on the now empty chair.

                    CAPTAIN
Here is my contract. I'll be here tomorrow at this
same time to retrieve the signed copy.

                    SUNNY JACK
Doesn't it require two signatures?

                    CAPTAIN
I've already signed it.

                    SUNNY JACK
So you're that sure there are no changes?

                    CAPTAIN
There will be no changes. I'm certain you'll find
everything to your liking.

                    SUNNY JACK
And if I don't?

                    CAPTAIN
I'll be here tomorrow regardless.

                    SUNNY JACK picks up the paperwork,
                    thumbs it.

                    SUNNY JACK
I need to show it to my attorney.

                    CAPTAIN
Of course. Still, there will be no changes. Goodbye,
Mr. Fennigan.

                    SUNNY JACK tips his head to the
                    man as CAPTAIN steps out.

                    Returning, SUNNY JACK paces with
                    the contract in his hand. At
                    last, he gets an odd look, a

nervous look. He stuffs the
contract quickly into the cabinet
and shuts the drawer.

He rests by the phone.

Behind him, the bathroom door
slowly opens.

Unseen by SUNNY JACK, PRETTY SEXY
appears in the motel bathroom
doorframe. She wears a
terrifyingly plain mask that
covers her face.

SOUND: A pulse sound, low in
frequency.

                    SUNNY JACK
Have you ever had heard that song, Pretty Sexy? I
mean--

He turns and startles.

She stands completely still.

He reaches out to take the mask
off her face when—

SOUND: The pulse builds, stronger,
more mechanical.

From behind the bed, MATCHBOX's
face appears.

SUNNY JACK sees this ghost and
freezes.

Slowly, from under the bed, crawls
THE VIL, covered in blood all over
white clothes.

SUNNY JACK backs towards the door.

PRETTY SEXY steps out of the doorframe, towards the telephone.

SOUND: The telephone begins ringing. No one answers.

SUNNY JACK opens the motel room door and bolts.

The three girls vanish inside the scene and the sound quiets.

Lights down.

ACT II

SCENE 3

Slow rise on THE VIL as she lays flat on the mattress. She still wears her blood-covered clothes. She seems to be waking from a nightmare. Suddenly, she jumps out of bed, shaking.

She looks down, sees the blood. She starts to examine it, pulling the hem to her eyes. This is not her blood, but someone else's.

She exits into the bathroom.

SOUND: Running water.

From the motel room door, CAPTAIN quietly enters and sits on the mattress. He sets his toolbox beside him. He opens it and takes out his radio from within and switches it on.

SOUND: White noise.

THE VIL hears this, turns off the water, and then emerges from the bathroom, freezing when she sees CAPTAIN on her bed.

CAPTAIN's radio speaks to her through the static.

                    CAPTAIN
          (Over radio)
I'm impressed. I read about you in the newspapers today. Six this time. I thought it may be too many. You're very talented. As I knew you would be.

                    THE VIL
Go away.

                    CAPTAIN
              (Over radio)
Why would I do *that*?

                    CAPTAIN approaches her. He lifts
                    her bloody dress up over her
                    panties, stopping at just below
                    her breasts, then lifts it fully
                    off. He touches the center of her
                    chest, where there's a bit of
                    splatter left.

                    CAPTAIN (Continued)
              (Over radio)
Go take a shower.

                    She exits to bathroom.

                    Lights fade. The white noise
                    continues, until...

ACT II

SCENE 4

Flash: a picture on the wall.
Another. Another, in another
spot. Faster and faster, to
strobes.

Sudden stop to blackout.

Blazing white light accompanied
by:

SOUND: A woman screaming offstage.

Sudden stop to blackout.

ACT II

SCENE 5

Lights rise to PRETTY SEXY in the
motel room, sleeping.

She wakes up suddenly, shakes off
a dream.

She goes to the corner and turns
on a lamp.

She sits near the bathroom and
stares out. After a long pause...

                    PRETTY SEXY
I know you're here. I can tell when you come. I've
always had a sense for that. Why do you wear a mask
sometimes? I get the feeling that it isn't your face.
It's the face of another. Who am I supposed to be
afraid of? Somehow... I don't think it's you.
          (Pause)
You can come out.
          (Pause, then singsong)
Come out, come out, wherever you are...

                    SOUND: Vibrations, continuing.

                    Out from under the bed, comes THE
                    VIL. She is covered in blood,
                    only in panties.

                    PRETTY SEXY turns and sees her
                    friend. She does not seem
                    frightened by this event.

                    THE VIL
I miss you.

                    PRETTY SEXY
I miss you, too. You're dead, right? This isn't some
kind of nightmare?

                    THE VIL
Matchbox warned me... that I would die. I came to
warn you, too.

                    PRETTY SEXY begins to cry.

                    PRETTY SEXY
Why me?

                    THE VIL
You signed a contract.

                    PRETTY SEXY
I didn't sign anything!

                    THE VIL
Yes. You did.

                    PRETTY SEXY
You mean with Captain? But *you* didn't sign with him?

                    THE VIL nods.

                    THE VIL
I wanted it. I signed it. We all wanted it. I just
didn't tell you.

                    PRETTY SEXY
I didn't come to Hollywood to die! I came here to
live *forever*!

                              SOUND and LIGHTS: Sudden swell of
                              cacophonic jazz horns to complete
                              blackout. Horns fade into car
                              horns and traffic.

                              Lights rise on PRETTY SEXY,
                              wandering lost in upstage
                              spotlights, hysterical.

PRETTY SEXY (Continued)
Don't leave! Don't leave me! I didn't sign a
contract! I'll tear it up!
          (Aside)
Fuck you -- I know, I know. It's MY street, too.
Fuck YOU!
          (To the air)
Fuck you, Hollywood! Do you want to see my tits! My
grandma's dead! Everyone I know is deeeeaaaad!

                    Blackout.

                    Long pause in total darkness.

                    In a nearby corner, a flashlight
                    comes on. It shines on the face
                    of the person who holds it: PRETTY
                    SEXY, eye makeup smeared and
                    running in tears. She continues
                    to weep and listens to the
                    silence.

                    SOUND: Rattles.

                    PRETTY SEXY (Continued)
Please go away... please. I want you to go away.
Please... please... please... please...

                    SOUND: Softly, bubblegum pop.

                    She cries fiercely and quickly.
                    Suddenly, the flashlight is swept
                    from her face and covered by her
                    hand.

                    Long pause.

                    When the light comes back to her
                    face, she wears a distorted mask,
                    a horrific image, funhouse and
                    strange.

The flashlight goes out.

SOUND: A hissing; Music fades.

ACT II

SCENE 6

Lights rise on the motel room.

The doorknob turns. Pause. A key in the
lock.

Enter SUNNY JACK.

He considers leaving the door open. At
last, he shuts it. He paces, wanders.

                    SUNNY JACK
I regret running. I should have stayed with all of you. It was
a missed opportunity, to see the three of you all together in
one spot. Even if... like that. I think you were trying to
tell me something.
          (Pause)
I'm across town now. If you're listening. Hyatt West
Hollywood. To be honest, it's... not for me. Full of junkie
musicians from the Strip. But, I suppose one motel room is like
another.
          (Pause)
Are you here? Are you?

                    SUNNY JACK bends and, hesitantly, inspects
                    under the bed. Then behind it. Nothing, no
                    one.

                    The bathroom door is shut.

                    He walks towards it.

                    SUNNY JACK (Continued)
You're not going to jump out and scare me, are you? You *like*
old Sunny Jack, right? I'm counting on that. Vil? Match?
Sexy?

                    No answer.

Slowly, he approaches the bathroom door.
Gaining courage, he opens it slowly to
reveal...

A rope around her neck, PRETTY SEXY dangles
several feet of the ground.

SUNNY JACK (Continued)
No, no, no!

He struggles and brings her down. He lays
her on the bed and unwraps the rope.

He checks her pulse.

She's dead.

He pulls away.

SUNNY JACK (Continued)
You did it. You did it. You idiot! You were the last one who
could help me. Were you too scared? Goddamnit!
          (Breaks down)
Oh, girls, girls, girls. I let you down, didn't I? I ruined
you. I opened the door to this motel room and let you all...
          (Shakes her body)
Wake up! Wake up! This isn't a goddamn audition!
          (Collapsing)
Wake up! Wake up! Wake up...
          (Whispering)
Please let me wake up.

Pause.

SOUND: A knock at the door.

Pause.

SOUND: Another knock.

The door opens on its own.

For a long moment, no one is there, until...

CAPTAIN steps from the darkness of the
unseen corridor into the doorway. He wears
no mask, carries no briefcase or radio or
toolbox.

He enters, each step a slow, agonizing
drawl.

He sees PRETTY SEXY, dead on the bed. He
sits with her and caresses her hair.

SUNNY JACK (Continued)
Get your fucking hands off her.

CAPTAIN smiles. He reaches between her
legs.

SUNNY JACK grabs CAPTAIN's hand and shoves
it away.

SUNNY JACK (Continued)
She's dead! She's dead, can't you see that, you-- You! What
are you? No. I want to know. You're not a man. You show me
all your goddamn photographs. The people you handle. You don't
handle them at all. You do *this*. You tricked me. Your fucking
contract. What are you! Stand up. Get up. What are you! Are
you the Devil? Answer me!

CAPTAIN
I'm not the Devil, Mr. Fennigan. But we do run in the same
social circles.

CAPTAIN begins to softly sing the bubblegum
pop song.

SUNNY JACK
Shut up! Shut up! Your shit doesn't work on me. I see through
you. I see right through your head! This is my motel room!

CAPTAIN
Is it?

75

                          SUNNY JACK
I'm calling the cops.

                              SUNNY JACK crosses to telephone, picks up
                              the receiver.

                              Suddenly, PRETTY SEXY jumps up from the bed
                              and screams, straight upright.

                              SUNNY JACK fumbles and drops the phone. He
                              stares at her.

                              CAPTAIN stands.

                              CAPTAIN
Kill him.
          (Pause)
Kill him.
          (Pause)
Kill. Him.

                              PRETTY SEXY takes a step.

                              Another.

                              Another.

                              SOUND: The telephone's off-the-hook signal
                              starts.

                              PRETTY SEXY looks infinitely sad.
                              At last, she moves forward and starts to
                              choke SUNNY JACK. With great strength, she
                              pushes him against the wall, the telephone
                              still in his hand.

                              SUNNY JACK, at first, does not resist. He
                              doesn't want to hurt her; he's too stunned
                              at what's happening. But slowly, he comes
                              to realize...

                              He frees a hand and wraps the phone cord
                              around PRETTY SEXY's neck and pulls and
                              pulls. After a moment, she slackens and

slides to the floor, dead again with the
phone around her, still buzzing.

SUNNY JACK hangs up the telephone just to
stop the sound.

                    CAPTAIN
Who's killed her now, Mr. Fennigan? You. Call the police.

Flashes of light begin. The film is
starting once more. The images are severe,
awful, increasing in speed and frequency.

                    SUNNY JACK
I want out of here. I want out.

                    CAPTAIN
This motel is yours. You said it yourself. Outside that door
is motel after motel after motel. And they all look like this
very room.

                    SUNNY JACK
You're telling me... what's out there is the same as what's in
here? No.

                    CAPTAIN
It's all the same. It's Hollywood.

SOUND: A building, blazing noise.

Strobes, blackouts, strobes again.

In the darkest seconds, CAPTAIN is gone from
the room.

SUNNY JACK runs to the motel room door. It
is shut, locked; he can't escape.

He runs to the bathroom door. It slams in
his face.

He circles around, trapped, panicked.

At last, in the noise and blare, resigned,
he sits on the bed. Lays down.

77

He pulls <u>a box of matches</u> from his jacket.

From the wall, PRETTY SEXY rises from the dead. She crosses in the noise and crawls onto the bed.

SUNNY JACK welcomes her beside him.

From behind the bed, MATCHBOX emerges. She lays at SUNNY JACK's feet.

At last, THE VIL emerges from underneath the bed and, with a look between her and SUNNY JACK of resignation, she joins him on the bed, coming close and sleeping softly.

Flashes turn red, the color of flames, orange and...

SOUND: A fire overtakes the other noises.

Blackout.

Final Curtain.

SOURCES

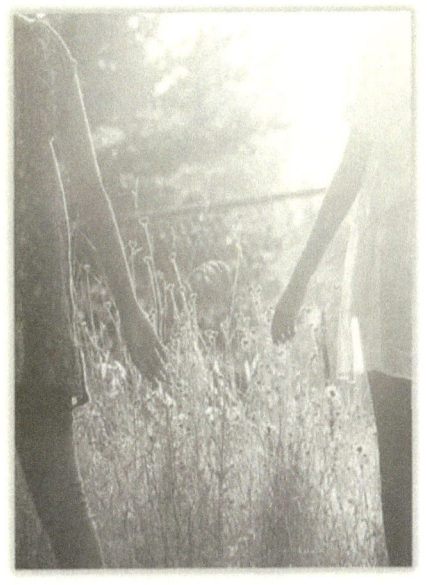

CAST OF CHARACTERS (in order of appearance)

(14 actors)

     KATHERINE LYMAN, an older woman

     SIENNA LYMAN, a younger woman

     ZOEY LYMAN, a younger woman

     REBECCA LYMAN, a younger woman

     CONNOR LYMAN, an older man

     JOHN HARBOUR, a man

     DAISY DILLINGER, a younger woman

     CHURCHYARD, an older man

     ARCHIE ANDERS, an older man

     DAVID WOLFF, a man

     CARBON COPY, referring to <u>two</u> individuals who are nearly identical

     TWO FILM VAMPIRES, females

The following may be combined for a smaller cast:

(7 actors)

     SIENNA LYMAN | DAISY DILLINGER | COPY

     CONNOR LYMAN | CHURCHYARD | DAVID WOLFF

     JOHN HARBOR | ARCHIE ANDERS

     ZOEY | VAMPIRE TWO

     Others would be the same as in the larger cast listing.

THE SETTING

Hollywood, California in the mid-1970s.

THE SCENE

The home of the Lyman family, a bedroom, an office, a pier, Daisy Dillinger's apartment, the home of Archie Anders, David Wolff's apartment, and a warehouse.

Exits stage right and stage left.

A NOTE ON FILM AND MEDIA

There are several films shown during the play. It is the director's discretion as to whether these are shown realistically or abstractly.

ACT I

SCENE 1

A 8mm film plays against a screen
in the empty living room of the
Lyman home. The film is a
document of a family vacation in
the 1960s, showing the pleasant
contentment between a husband,
wife, and three young daughters.

As the film plays, the LYMANS
enter from various points. These
are the people in the film, now
older. The girls are grown and
each dressed as smartly as their
parents.

The mother, KATHERINE LYMAN, wears
a white dress and reclines in a
chair. She smokes a cigarette
through a filter.

REBECCA LYMAN sways; she is
pregnant.

SIENNA LYMAN lightly pats her
hair-sprayed 'do. She wears a
tight sweater and Capri pants.

ZOEY LYMAN blows bubbles with her
chewing gum.

And the father, CONNOR LYMAN,
mixes a cocktail at the bar.

The film holds on a young woman --
SIENNA, as a child. Luminescent.
The camera loves her, even then.

The film tapers off.

Lights rise.

                        CONNOR
Tahoe?

                        The women groan.

                        CONNOR (Continued)
Don't you...? I mean, Katherine, help me here.

                        KATHERINE
I'm out.

                        CONNOR
On a mission.

                        KATHERINE
You drag that machine from the closet every holiday.
I have limits.

                        ZOEY
Bravo, Mother!

                        KATHERINE
Nostalgia is never good, or have you forgotten?
What's past is past. I like focusing on 'now.' To be
reminded that I was young, and that you all have grown
up beyond my reach, is too depressing.

                        SIENNA gives KATHERINE a warm hug.

                        SIENNA
Not beyond your reach, Mother.

                        KATHERINE
Please, Sienna, all that hair spray.

                        SIENNA
I like watching those old movies. Don't ever stop,
Dad. When I see them, I have the best memories. I
remember things that aren't on the screen, things that
happened off of it. Things that weren't caught, but
were good, and should be remembered. All those
possibilities.

                    CONNOR
Possibilities. You're twenty. You've got an
abundance of possibilities.

                    SIENNA
I know. It's just that I want to remember everything,
everything... everything.

                    ZOEY
You like watching them because you're beautiful.

                    KATHERINE
You're *all* beautiful.

          CONNOR touches SIENNA's shoulder.

                    CONNOR
Your mother's right. You are and forever will be
beautiful.

                    REBECCA
Only one of us is in the movie business.

          SIENNA struts.

                    SIENNA
          (Southern accent)
"I beg pardon; I didn't know it could get so hot in
Tennessee this time of the year. Perhaps Mr.
McGillicutty can spare a drink of his cool, cool
water."

                    The girls laugh as SIENNA
                    stretches for a drink at the bar,
                    showing her legs.

                    KATHERINE
Eh, eh... Remember: you are being watched.

                    SIENNA
          (Southern accent)

Can't an ingénue have a little ol' drink?

> Sienna giggles and puts down the
> drink.

CONNOR
I like my daughter away from the Devil.

REBECCA
Here in California? You should know by now, father,
that's just not possible.

KATHERINE
When a brassiere becomes too quaint, and there are
films about real life and real problems, you know
trying to protect Sienna from *anything* is pointless.
I've taught you well, Sienna. One small role as a
southern trollop won't turn you to salt.

SIENNA
We should all go together to the red carpet.

ZOEY
How many tickets did they give you?

SIENNA
Two. But I can get more. My agent has a connection.
He wants me to take a handsome boy, but I'd much
rather take all of you.

CONNOR
Better stick with the boy. Papers can be cruel.

SIENNA
They won't even care. They'll think I'm one of the
crew. The jezebel is a small part. You oversell my
success.

KATHERINE
Photographers always notice a pretty girl. They can
recognize a future.

SIENNA
I've seen you be a little grand, mother, from time to
time. But now you claim clairvoyance?

                         KATHERINE
               (Dramatic)
Alas, I have no magic. I am a mere mortal on this
fatal plane, looking for answers, just the same.

               SIENNA considers.

                         SIENNA
Speaking of magic... Do you want to see something? I
wasn't going to show you this, *but*...
               (Pause)
Well, do you want to see or not?

                         REBECCA
What is it?

                         SIENNA
Something I learned.

                         REBECCA
Show off.

                         ZOEY
Shhhh. Let her do it.

                         CONNOR
No more summersaults on the lawn. That pervert next
door enjoys it too much.

                         SIENNA
Not a summersault.

                         KATHERINE
As long as I don't have to move from this chair... I'm
sotted and comfortable. Cocooned. You around me. A
Sunday before dark. When there's just a little light
in the air and everyone is as they should be.
               (Catching herself)
Like I said: nostalgia is never good.

                        SIENNA crosses to the table. She
                        removes objects from the table and
                        sets them on the floor.

                        KATHERINE (Continued)
I hope you are planning to put those back.

                        SIENNA smiles sheepishly and
                        continues her preparations.

                        She places a hand flat over the
                        table, but then stops suddenly.

                        SIENNA
Wait, wait. I forgot something.

                        SIENNA dims the lights.

                        REBECCA
Grrr, no, not another Super 8.

                        SIENNA returns to the table with a
                        dismissive wave.

                        SIENNA
Okay, promise you won't laugh.

                        Hand across the table, SIENNA
                        slowly opens her fingers.

                        A <u>light</u> emanates from under her
                        hand. Though it looks simple, <u>the
                        trick is stunning</u>.

                        SIENNA closes her hand and the
                        light dies, like she's snuffed a
                        candle.

                        The room holds in darkness.

SIENNA goes to the switch.

Lights on, SIENNA notes the
expressions on the faces of the
others.

                    SIENNA (Continued)
Did you like it?

ZOEY snatches SIENNA's hand.

                    ZOEY
          (Excited)
How did you *do* that? Let me see.

There is nothing in Sienna's hand.

                    SIENNA
It's a trick.

KATHERINE rises and stubs out her
cigarette, thoughtful.

                    KATHERINE
How was it done?

                    SIENNA
It's a trick.

                    KATHERINE
Yes, you said that. Tell us what you did.

                    REBECCA
She's not supposed to give away the trick. That's bad
magic.

SIENNA looks to her father.

                    SIENNA
Dad. It was just a trick. Didn't you like it?
                    CONNOR
Who taught you that?

                    SIENNA
I thought you'd be amused.

                    ZOEY
It was wonderful! Will you teach me?

                    SIENNA
I promised I'd keep it to myself.

                    REBECCA
It was a little creepy.

                    SIENNA
Oh, come on. It was a trick!
          (Defensive)
Well, I'm sorry I showed it to you now.

                    KATHERINE
It's something simple, right? Something we'll laugh
about. A mirror and, and a flashlight.

                         REBECCA crosses to SIENNA and
                         inspects her pockets. She
                         examines the underside of the
                         table.

                    REBECCA
Mom's right. Isn't she? It's something easy.

                    SIENNA
I didn't mean to scare you.

                         SIENNA starts to put the items
                         back on top of the table.

8

KATHERINE

I'm not scared. I don't think. I don't want you to
do that ever again.

SIENNA

Mom, it's just a trick.

KATHERINE
            (Quiet)
I know, I know.

> An awkward moment passes. CONNOR
> downs his drink. ZOEY looks
> confused.
>
> SIENNA checks the time.

SIENNA

Oh, shoot. Look, I have to get going.

> SIENNA gathers her things.

SIENNA (Continued)

I wasn't kidding about red carpet. I'll see what I
can arrange. My agent -- he has to do me favors,
right? That's part of the job. I can't do *all* the
work. He has me running around Hollywood meeting the
craziest people. He owes me. Will you come?

KATHERINE

For certain.

SIENNA

Great.
            (Pause)
Really. It was just a trick. I thought you'd laugh.

CONNOR

It was a good trick.

KATHERINE

Yes. A good trick. But I don't want to see it again.

                        SIENNA
Okay.   I love you.

                        SIENNA exits with awkwardness.

                        Lights down.

ACT I

SCENE 2

KATHERINE LYMAN's bedroom. She is
sleeping. She wears a black
dress.

ZOEY enters in the darkness.

                    ZOEY
          (Soft)
Mom. Mother. You have to get up.

                    KATHERINE
Sienna?

                    ZOEY
          (Disappointed)
No. It's Zoey. You have to get up. They're starting
to arrive.

                    KATHERINE
What time is it?

                    ZOEY
It's almost two.

                    KATHERINE
Did I fall asleep?

                    ZOEY
Yes. For just a few minutes. I thought you were
fixing your makeup.

                         ZOEY gently pulls her mother out
                         of bed and draws her from the
                         bedroom into the living room.

                         Lights rise as she enters.

                         REBECCA stands at the bar,
                         drinking. She is no longer
                         pregnant. She wears a black
                         dress.

Two others are in the room...

JOHN HARBOUR: tall, in a black suit.

DAISY DILLINGER: blonde, in a black dress.

                    KATHERINE
Who are these people?

                    ZOEY
Mom...

                    KATHERINE
Who are they?

                    HARBOUR
We met several times, Mrs. Lyman. First by phone.
You saw me earlier this morning. The cemetery?

KATHERINE looks blank.

                    HARBOUR (Continued)
I'm John Harbour.

                    ZOEY
          (Whisper)
Sienna's agent.
          (With gesture)
And Daisy.

DAISY fans an uncomfortable wave.

                    ZOEY (Continued)
          (Embarrassed)
Mom. You met these people. You *know* who they are.

                    KATHERINE
We met at, at the cemetery?

                    KATHERINE, lost, wanders her
                    house.

                    KATHERINE (Continued)
Where's Connor?   Where's my husband?

                    HARBOUR comes forward and takes
                    Katherine's hand.

                    HARBOUR
I should go. Please know, Mrs. Lyman, that if there's
any help you or your daughters need, anything at all,
you can reach me at my office. Here's my card. I'm
there most days after three o'clock. And I will
certainly let you know if there is any word from
Sienna.

                    KATHERINE
Where is she?

                    Awkward gazes pass.

                    HARBOUR
Good day, Mrs. Lyman. My deepest condolences.

                    He exits.

                    DAISY, without asking, starts a
                    drink at the bar.

                    KATHERINE
No! Don't! My husband makes the drinks around here.

                    DAISY stops, but on a gesture from
                    REBECCA continues.

                                                        13

                    KATHERINE (Continued)
Please, someone tell me. I've woken from a bad dream.
Or maybe I'm still in it.

                         REBECCA
Mother! How dare you! After everything! How dare
you lose it like this!

                         KATHERINE
After WHAT? After WHAT?
          (To ZOEY)
Tell me, Zoey. Please.

                         REBECCA runs from the room.

                         ZOEY comes forward and, for a
                         moment, looks sympathetically to
                         her mother.

                    KATHERINE (Continued)
What happened to Rebecca's baby?

                         ZOEY quickly exits.

                         DAISY remains. She shows no
                         emotion; she drinks.

                         DAISY
I was Sienna's roommate. She never mentioned me. You
didn't even know where she had been living. You told
me that bit at the funeral. You're losing it, aren't
you?

                         KATHERINE
Who has died? Tell me. Please.

                         DAISY
You really don't remember?

                         KATHERINE
The last thing I remember... We were watching home
movies. Just a few hours ago. Sienna had to leave.

14

                      DAISY
Sienna's been missing for five weeks.

                  KATHERINE
What?

                      DAISY
Yeah. The police are trying to find her.

                  KATHERINE
Five weeks?

                      DAISY
You filed a report. A missing person's.

                  KATHERINE
I did?

                      DAISY
Sure. What, you go and lose your mind or somethin'?

                  KATHERINE retreats to her bedroom
                  and lies down. After a moment,
                  DAISY puts down her drink, thinks,
                  and then follows.

                 DAISY (Continued)
You think you're in a dream? You're not. I don't
want to be mean. This sounds mean, doesn't it? I
just want you to know the score.
        (Pause)
Listen, I'm going...

                  KATHERINE
        (To pillow)
Get my husband. Please.

                      DAISY
He's dead.

                  KATHERINE
Connor?

DAISY

You were there. You said stuff at the church. You dropped a flower in the hole.

KATHERINE

FUCK YOU, YOU CUNT!

DAISY

Look, I didn't even want to be here! I had plans.

KATHERINE

Then *get out*!

> DAISY returns to the bar. She drinks.
>
> KATHERINE rises, limp, and props herself against the bedroom door.

KATHERINE (Continued)

If it's true... then why can't I remember? It is like there's a big, blank spot I can't see around. I... I don't easily forget things... but I've forgotten so much...

DAISY

Did you take a pill? You've been drinking. Something to calm the nerves. Maybe they don't mix.

KATHERINE

But how can I not remember five *weeks*? A kind of drug like that. I feel like I've been hypnotized. Are you acting? Are you all playing a joke? Tell me that's true. I need to hear it. How can I forget everything so completely?

DAISY

Crazy business, isn't it? Well maybe it's best to forget. You just go and lie down, Mrs. Lyman. I'm sure someone will be back for you soon.
          (Pause)
Go on. Lie down. I didn't come to baby-sit.

                    KATHERINE
I don't need a stranger to tell me my husband's dead.

                    DAISY
I saw the notice in the paper. And I guess I wondered
if Sienna was gonna surprise us. Her dad's funeral –
you would think that'd be worth an appearance. People
don't vanish that much. At least not in my life. I
guess I was kind of curious.

                    KATHERINE
Sienna was here, this afternoon. Just a few hours
ago.

                    DAISY
Was she now?

                    KATHERINE
She was, she was! It, it COULDN'T have been five
weeks. She was here. And she did some sort of a
magic trick.

                    DAISY
Ha. She couldn't tie her shoes. I doubt she was any
good with rabbits.

                              DAISY thinks on this. At last,
                              she pours a second drink and hands
                              it to KATHERINE.

                    DAISY (Continued)
Get drunk.

                    KATHERINE
I'm scared.

                    DAISY
I know. Get drunk.

                    KATHERINE
Do *you* know what's happened to my daughter? You must.
                    (MORE)

                    KATHERINE (Continued)
You... you know what happened. If she walks into the
room now, I'll think it was a good joke. I won't be
mad. I know actors like to play pranks.

                    DAISY
Got a cigarette?

                    KATHERINE
I think so...

                            KATHERINE finds a pack. For the
                            first time, she notices she is
                            wearing a black dress.

                    KATHERINE (Continued)
There is mud on my shoes.

                    DAISY
Yes, it was raining at the grave.

                            KATHERINE swallows her drink.

                    DAISY (Continued)
That's it. Get drunk.

                            KATHERINE fumbles with her
                            cigarette. Daisy holds out her
                            lighter, strikes it.

                    KATHERINE
I need my filters.

                    DAISY
Doesn't matter.

                            The cigarette is lit.

DAISY (Continued)

Here. Another drink.

KATHERINE

What was your name again? Daisy?

DAISY

That's right.

KATHERINE

Zoey and Rebecca abandoned me. Why are you being kind?

DAISY

Sienna said you were worth it.

KATHERINE

How long did you know her?

DAISY

A couple months.

KATHERINE

Were you friends?

DAISY

I'm not sure you could say that. We lived together to stretch the rent. It was an arrangement.

KATHERINE

Do you know where she is?

DAISY toasts KATHERINE's glass.

DAISY

I do not. But I know where she isn't.

KATHERINE

Where's that?

DAISY

Anywhere near the obituaries.

Lights fade.

ACT I

SCENE 3

JOHN HARBOUR's office.

Desk and a chair.

A film poster hangs on the wall:
Hunt Her, Kill Her (a woman in the
woods, half-naked, sweaty –
obviously an exploitation film; no
text other than the title.)

HARBOUR compulsively straightens.

SOUND: A soft knock at the door.

HARBOUR listens, paces. He
answers the door to find KATHERINE
waiting.

                    HARBOUR
Mrs. Lyman!

                    KATHERINE enters.

                    HARBOUR takes her arm and escorts
                    her to the chair.

                    HARBOUR (Continued)
You came. That's terrific. Please. Be comfortable.
Sunday you didn't seem yourself. Not that I'm blaming
you. Terrible day. Funerals! But I'm glad you're
here. I should have warned you: this place is *below*
respectable. Did you spot the drunks down the street,
in front of the liquor window? I come here to answer
the phone and check messages. Rest of the time I'm at
the lots, or auditions. So. Are you feeling better?

                    KATHERINE
Better?

HARBOUR

I understand. It's a relative state. You're probably
not anywhere near your capacity. But are you better
than the last time we spoke?

KATHERINE

I've lost my memory.

HARBOUR

Hmmmm. Mem-mor-ry...

KATHERINE

I remember Sienna's visit to the house five weeks ago.
Then... Sunday.

HARBOUR

Oh... Christ. That's terrible. Have you seen a
doctor?

KATHERINE

I have. He was no help.

HARBOUR

Well. Jeez. Tragedies like you've been through.
Piled up and up. Memory gives you a break. Maybe not
the one you wanted. Suppose it's like... going into a
coma. Self-preservation of a sort.

KATHERINE

That was the doctor's theory. Do you want to hear
mine?

HARBOUR

...Of course.

KATHERINE

I was drugged.

HARBOUR
(Taken aback)
Heh... Well. Well, well, well. I—

KATHERINE

Nothing "well" about it. Between a few conversations,
(MORE)

                    KATHERINE (Continued)
I've been able to piece together what has happened.
Sienna vanished two days after I last saw her. I
spent the next few weeks putting up posters, driving
up and down Sunset, making telephone calls. I don't
remember doing any of this... but I've learned it.
And, you've been helping as well.

                         HARBOUR
As I could, yes. Sienna was one of my rising meal
tickets. But it's not all mercenary; I liked her,
too. She was a real doll.

                         KATHERINE
And then my oldest, Rebecca, had a miscarriage at
near-term. Just about four weeks ago. And then my
husband of twenty-two years dies of a massive heart
attack. He didn't even have a heart condition. Isn't
that strange?

                         HARBOUR
Like I said. Piled up, up... up. You're due for a
turn in luck.

                         KATHERINE
Do you believe she's alive?

                         HARBOUR
I do. Sure. Certainly.

                         KATHERINE
That's the most optimistic reply yet.

                         HARBOUR
You and I see Sienna the same, Mrs. Lyman. A little
girl wearing put-on costumes and makeup, mugging in
front of the mirror. I pushed her onto the callback
lines. Held her sweaty palms and listened to her
nervous laughs. And when she got that part in
"Southern Rhapsody," we both knew it was the start of
something. Dreamers don't stop. They keep going,
despite the odds. Despite rejection. Am I making you
uncomfortable?

                         KATHERINE
What?

                    HARBOUR
It's just that you look nervous.

                    KATHERINE
That movie.   The poster.

                    HARBOUR eyes the poster for *Hunt
                    Her, Kill Her.*

                    HARBOUR
Was a gift.

                    KATHERINE
Is it a real film?

                    HARBOUR
Sure.   Why not?

                    KATHERINE
I've never heard of it.

                    HARBOUR
Lots of films never get heard of.   This town makes a
hundred a month.   The public sees about a tenth of
those.   The others get buried.   Never seen this one
myself.   Buddy of mine pushed me to make my crappy
office more Hollywood and that's what he could spare.
I'm just glad it wasn't a comedy.   Hate comedies.
Dramas.   Thrillers.   Westerns are okay.   You like
movies, Mrs. Lyman?

                    KATHERINE
I used to.

                    HARBOUR
Holy Moses.   Stand up.

                    KATHERINE
I-

                    HARBOUR
Stand up.

                    She obeys.   He circles her.

                    HARBOUR (Continued)
Let me think. Thinking here. Matron. Possibly a
church. I'm seeing a church. Is that right?

                    KATHERINE
I don't know what you're talking about.

                    HARBOUR
A scene. From a film. Getting flashes. No, wait,
wait. Not a church. A museum. You played... I can
see it. The tour guide. Yes, that's it, the tour
guide at the Metropolitan Museum in one of those
Archie Anders films. See: my special talent!

                    KATHERINE
I'm not an actor.

                    HARBOUR
You're kidding me. You see, I have this crazy mind.
I see something once and it sticks with me. Never
forget a face. You sure you weren't in the Anders
flick?

                    KATHERINE
I'm certain.

                    HARBOUR
Oh. Then I made a boo-boo.

                    KATHERINE
So you have no special talents?

                    HARBOUR
You're the first one I've gotten wrong. But I'm gonna
check your resume, Mrs. Lyman. I think you're pullin'
my leg.
          (Considering)
Am I talking too much? I haven't even asked why
you've come to see me. Here, making you stand! I'm
such a jerk. Please, be comfortable. Ah, I don't
have anything to offer you. Water? You want water?
There's a fountain in the hall. I think I've got some
paper cups...

                    HARBOUR rifles the desk.

                    KATHERINE
Mr. Harbour: what do you know about magic tricks?

                    HARBOUR stops cold.

                    HARBOUR
Magic tricks?

                    KATHERINE
Yes.

                    HARBOUR
Knowing faces - that's not a magic trick.

                    KATHERINE
I'm talking about something with light.

                    HARBOUR
Light? What's this got to do with-?

                    KATHERINE
Sienna, she did a magic trick. She held her hand over
a table and her hand glowed. It was very real. We
were all there. It was the last time I saw her. None
of it made any sense. We don't know how she did it.

                    HARBOUR
I don't handle any magicians. I'm sorry. Did you
tell the police about this trick?

                    KATHERINE
Apparently I didn't. Not at first. I checked. I
just told them this morning and they didn't believe
me.

                    HARBOUR's hand has not left the
                    desk drawer.

                    KATHERINE (Continued)
Did *you* teach her this trick?

                                                      25

                    HARBOUR
No. No, I didn't.

                    KATHERINE
Do you know who might have?

                    HARBOUR
I didn't know all Sienna's friends, Mrs. Lyman. Only
some.

                    KATHERINE
Were any of them magicians?

                    HARBOUR
I don't think so. No. I don't think so... not... not
that I can rec—

                    KATHERINE
Have you found that paper cup yet?

                    HARBOUR looks at his arm, in the
                    desk. His face twitches, nervous.

                    Slowly, he pulls a pistol from his
                    desk.

                    He points it at KATHERINE for just
                    a second, his face turning
                    serious; he then has a change of
                    heart.

                    HARBOUR
Prop gun. Doesn't even work. Did I scare you?

                    KATHERINE stands.

                    KATHERINE
I should be going.

                    HARBOUR, with the pistol, comes
                    around and blocks the door.

HARBOUR

Look, I'm an agent. That's all. That's all I was for
Sienna. I got her work. "Southern Rhapsody." That
was me. I got her that audition.

KATHERINE

I've got to go.

HARBOUR

You can't go. I can see it: you don't believe me.

KATHERINE

It's not about believing you. You seem strange. I
don't think I should stay.

HARBOUR

My reputation is built on trust. People trust me.
Lots of people. You can ask them. You can use the
phone. I'll. I'll give you the number for the head
of casting at Warner's. He'll vouch for me. He will.
Heck, he probably can vouch for you, too... Warner's
made that museum picture, didn't they?

KATHERINE

I told you: that wasn't me. Now get out of my way.
Please.

HARBOUR

You can use the phone.
          (Pause)
See? It's right there.

                    Long pause. KATHERINE looks
                    behind her to the phone on the
                    desk.

                    KATHERINE
          (Cautiously)
All right.

                    She backs to the phone.

27

                    KATHERINE (Continued)
What's the number?

                    HARBOUR chews on the barrel of the
                    pistol, nervous.

                    HARBOUR
          (Through teeth)
Seven four seven…

                    KATHERINE dials. Pause.

                    HARBOUR (Continued)
Eight...

                    KATHERINE spins the eight.

                    HARBOUR looks a wreck. He rests
                    the gun at his waist.

                    HARBOUR (Continued)
I don't know anything about any trick.

                    KATHERINE
Then who does?

                    Pause.

                    HARBOUR
          (Quickly)
Two eight seven six eleven.

                    Katherine finishes dialing.

                    An audible ring on the other side.
                    A second ring.

HARBOUR comes forward and presses
the cancel.

Their eyes meet.

He grabs her and puts the pistol
in her stomach. His face is ticks
and twitches.

She does not fight him.

                KATHERINE
          (Soft)
Mr. Harbour? Mr. Harbour? John. *Is* that a prop gun?

He fires until the pistol is
empty.

KATHERINE stands before him,
unharmed.

Realizing it is, in fact, a prop,
KATHERINE falls over the desk and
runs at the door.

HARBOUR catches her.

They fight.

KATHERINE's hand finds the
telephone. She hits HARBOUR over
and over on the head until he is
still.

SOUND: The phone's off the hook
signal buzzes, insistent.

Blood empties under HARBOUR's
head.

Lights and phone's signal fade.

ACT I

SCENE 4

HARBOUR's office, later.

Lights rise to dusk.

KATHERINE looks out the window,
smokes a cigarette, her back to
the audience.

HARBOUR's body lies on the floor,
just as before.

Lights fade.

ACT I

SCENE 5

HARBOUR's office, even later.

Lights rise to barely lit/night.

KATHERINE remains at the window, her cigarette now down to its filter.

HARBOUR's body is unchanged.

SOUND: A knock.

KATHERINE goes to the door, unbolts it, and then thinks better of it.

                    KATHERINE
Who's there?

                    REBECCA
          (Through door)
It's us, Mom.

                    She opens the door to REBECCA and
                    ZOEY.

                    The two daughters immediately
                    assess. ZOEY covers her mouth;
                    REBECCA bends towards HARBOUR's
                    body.

                    REBECCA
That's John Harbour!

                    KATHERINE
He attacked me.

                    ZOEY
Is he dead?

                    KATHERINE
Yes.

                    REBECCA rolls HARBOUR over and
                    inspects. When finished, she
                    stands, shaking. She wipes her
                    bloody fingers on her skirt.

                    KATHERINE (Continued)
What do we do?

                    REBECCA
You don't know?

                    ZOEY
We call the police.

                    KATHERINE
What if they don't believe us?

                    REBECCA
Us?

                    ZOEY comes around the desk, sees
                    the gun.

                    ZOEY
Is that a gun?

                    KATHERINE
It's not real. It's a prop. What if, what if they
think I killed him in confusion? I mean, maybe if the
gun was real-

                    REBECCA
Confusion? I mean, do we honestly know what happened
here today? He's an agent, Mom! He got Sienna *jobs*.
Why would he attack you?

KATHERINE

Stop. I know what you're implying, Rebecca. You
didn't see his eyes. He wanted to shut me up. He
wouldn't let me leave.

REBECCA

But why?

KATHERINE

Because I told him about the trick.

REBECCA

Oh, *Christ*, Mom. It was a stupid trick Sienna picked
up on the set.

KATHERINE

It wasn't some stupid trick! Everything was lovely
until that trick.

REBECCA

Everything was lovely. But you'd have found a way to
screw it up. You did before and did again tonight.

KATHERINE

Shut up. Don't talk to me in that voice.
          (To ZOEY)
You don't know how Sienna did that trick.

ZOEY

No, but it's not IMPORTANT!

KATHERINE

It is!
          (To REBECCA)
You don't know how she did it either! What's to say
it wasn't *more* than a parlor game? He wanted to kill
me. He did. He wanted to kill me because I mentioned
it.

REBECCA

What did he say *exactly*?

KATHERINE

I don't remember.

REBECCA

Oh, come ON, Mom!

                        KATHERINE
It's been two hours!

                        REBECCA
You only phoned us an hour ago. How could it—

                        KATHERINE
So blame me, then. I. I didn't know what to do.
Rebecca — you always expect so much of me.

                        REBECCA
No — I expect very little.

                         ZOEY
Please! Stop fighting. Let's get out of this first.
You two can pick at each other like crows another day.
Should we — should we call the police?

                        REBECCA
No, wait a minute. Let's think about this. You come
here and ask him about the trick, he pulls a gun on
you. The gun's not real. Did he know that?

                        KATHERINE
I think so. He was very disturbed. I don't think he
was right in the head. He seemed fine at first, but
then got stranger and stranger.

                        REBECCA
He attacks you and won't let you leave.

                        KATHERINE
Yes. I, I hit him with the telephone and he stopped
moving.

                         ZOEY
He must know *something* about Sienna.

                        ZOEY opens desk drawers.

                        ZOEY (Continued)
Did you search in here?

                         KATHERINE
No, I didn't want to touch anything.

                                   ZOEY pulls items from the desk.

                         ZOEY
Photographs.

                                   KATHERINE and REBECCA come around
                                   to inspect the stack. ZOEY fans
                                   the photographs on the desk.

                         KATHERINE
Actors. Probably clients.

                         ZOEY
               (Finding)
Sienna.

                                   KATHERINE holds up the photograph.
                                   After a long moment, she gently
                                   sets it back down. She notices
                                   something: another picture.

                         KATHERINE
Do you recognize her?

                         REBECCA
Isn't she-?

                         ZOEY
That girl from Connor's funeral.

                         KATHERINE
Daisy.
               (Reading)
Daisy Dillinger. Name and address. She didn't
mention she was an actress.

                         REBECCA
               (Thumbing pictures)
I don't recognize the rest. Do you?

                         ZOEY
                 (Pointing to a photograph)
What about her?

                         KATHERINE
I've never seen her before.

                         ZOEY
                 (Pointing to *Hunt Her, Kill Her*)
She's in that poster.

                         KATHERINE holds up the photograph.
                         She hesitates then decides.

                         KATHERINE
Take the pictures. All of them.

                         REBECCCA
Are we going to call the police?

                         KATHERINE
No. I'm beginning to think we shouldn't. If I see
doubt in my daughters, how do you think the police
will look at what's happened?

                         REBECCA
Let's get out of here. I'm getting the creeps.

                         ZOEY
                 (Pointing to HARBOUR)
What about him?

                         KATHERINE
Leave him. Leave him where he is.

                         REBECCA
Maybe we can call the police later. From a pay phone.
Tell them there's a body. Did you touch anything?

                         KATHERINE
What?

                         REBECCA
We should fix anything we've touched.

36

                    KATHERINE
The window.

                    ZOEY
I have a handkerchief.

                    REBECCA
I touched his clothes.

          ZOEY dusts the room.

          KATHERINE watches and then unhooks
          the telephone from the wall.

                    REBECCA
What are you going to do with that?

                    KATHERINE
We'll throw it off the pier.

                    REBECCA
Did you tell anyone you were coming here?

                    KATHERINE
No one.

                    REBECCA
Not even that Daisy?

                    KATHERINE
We should be okay.

                    REBECCA
Did anyone see you come in? Did anyone pass by in the
corridor?

                    KATHERINE
No. Wait. On the street, but that was after. I saw
two people across the way.

                    ZOEY
Did they notice you in the window?

37

                    KATHERINE
I don't think so. They were wearing coats. They just
stood there and when I looked again they were gone.

                    REBECCA
          (To ZOEY)
Hurry up. I want to get out of here.

                    ZOEY
          (Looking out window)
Street's clear.

                    REBECCA
Come on, Mom.

                         KATHERINE gazes a last time at
                         HARBOUR's body, the blood, then to
                         the telephone clutched in her
                         arms.

                    REBECCA (Continued)
Mother, come on!

                         KATHERINE snaps out of it. They
                         leave with ZOEY wiping the door.

                         Lights out.

ACT I

SCENE 6

The stage is clouded with fog.

In lowlight, KATHERINE, ZOEY, and
REBECCA cross.

Over a railing, KATHERINE heaves
the telephone.

SOUND: A splash of water.

                KATHERINE
Do phones float?

                ZOEY
What if we didn't clean good enough?

                REBECCA
Too late now. We need to think of an answer to every
question.

                KATHERINE
I'll say I went to his office, but that I left before
anything happened.

                REBECCA
No. You'll say you met me for dinner.

                ZOEY
Where?

                KATHERINE
        (Thinking)
The Reese Hotel.

                ZOEY
Yeah. Yeah.

                SOUND: Faraway police sirens,
                distant car horns.

                              REBECCA
                    (Turning KATHERINE to her)
          Tell me mother: what's your memory like now?

                              KATHERINE
          I wish I could forget everything about tonight.

                              REBECCA
          Me, too.

                              ZOEY
                    (Awe)
          You killed a man.

                              KATHERINE
          I killed a man.

                    KATHERINE collapses on the street.

                    Her daughters rouse her.

                              ZOEY
          Mom! Mom!

                    KATHERINE weeps.

                              ZOEY (Continued)
          Listen, listen, listen. It's okay. Mom, it's okay.

                    KATHERINE can't look at her
                    daughters.

                              KATHERINE
          We're never going to get away with this.

                              ZOEY
          No, no, we are. We are.

                              REBECCA
          I'm a young woman. I want to have a baby. I don't
          want to go to jail.

                    ZOEY
Shush!

                    REBECCA
The world doesn't revolve around the great Katherine
Lyman, you know. I have a life! Why is it always
your stupid choices that wreck us? First breaking
dad's heart and now-

                    ZOEY
Rebecca -- John Harbour attacked mom!

                    REBECCA
Did he? You know what she's like.

                    KATHERINE looks up.

                    REBECCA (Continued)
You know what I'm talking about.

                    KATHERINE tries to slap REBECCA,
                    but she catches her hand.

                    KATHERINE
Your father has just passed. Respect him.

                    REBECCA
Where was all your respect when he was alive?

                    ZOEY
Rebecca!

                    KATHERINE
I don't want your help. Go to the police.

                    REBECCA
No. I'm going to help you. I'm going to help you so
much it will hurt you. And you will *owe me* for all
the lies I've been through as your oldest. What's one
more lie, Mother? Zoey and Sienna knew about you and
your men, but they think it was a phase and it's done.
I know you better. This is just a lull.

                                                    41

                    KATHERINE
One day, you'll understand. I'm a better woman than
you think, Rebecca.

                    REBECCA
Prove it.

                    KATHERINE climbs to her feet.

                    KATHERINE
What about how you got that baby, then? You're not
perfect. You're no stranger to men, either. You
fallen for anyone who tells you there's something
better. You'll learn. Nothing's true in this town.

                    Lights fade.

ACT I

SCENE 7

Blackness.

SOUND: Katherine's voice on a
telephone.

KATHERINE
(Over phone)
It's Katherine Lyman. I'm coming to see you. I'll be
there at eight o'clock. I'm sorry if that's too
early. You'll understand when I get there. I'm
bringing my youngest. Zoey. You met her on Sunday.
I wasn't in the best condition Sunday, but I'm better
now. I won't be a burden. But I have to see you.
It's about Sienna. Please be home.

SOUND: Disconnect, fading into a
retro pop song.

Lights rise on DAISY's apartment
in morning-time.

It is spare, with sofa and a
switched-off television with
"rabbit ears."

Clothes pile on the floor, a
brassiere drapes across a chair,
which sets near a makeup table.

DAISY sits with her back to the
audience, listening to the song on
the radio. She wears only her
cotton panties. She pulls on
hosiery, a blouse, at last her
mini-skirt.

SOUND: Knocking.

DAISY answers to find KATHERINE
and ZOEY outside.

                        DAISY
You're twenty minutes late.

                        KATHERINE
I couldn't find the door. There's no number.

                        DAISY
It fell off.

                        KATHERINE
All these apartments look the same.

                        DAISY
Built for cheap, not for convenience. Come in.

                        They enter.

                        DAISY (Continued)
Pardon the mess.

                        ZOEY
Hello.

                        DAISY
I only have a few minutes.

                        KATHERINE
Have we made you late for work?

                        DAISY
No.

                        She lets the comment hang.

                        DAISY (Continued)
I don't have any coffee made. I'm sorry.

                        KATHERINE
I've been up all night. I don't think I've slept
in... in... I'm not sure.

44

                    DAISY
Still the forgetful type, huh? Can you help me with
the buttons?

                    DAISY turns. Her blouse needs
                    buttoned in the back. ZOEY steps
                    forward.

                    DAISY (Continued)
Sienna used to do this for me. I knew I could count
on a Lyman.

                    ZOEY finishes.

                    KATHERINE
I hope we can count on you, Daisy.

                    DAISY
A favor, huh? I knew it. I wondered how you got my
name and number. You must have good sources. First I
thought you were comin' to tell me some bad news about
Sienna. But then neither of you were cryin' when I
answered the door. Must be my face. People can't
hide a thing — they break like babies with stubbed
toes when it's bad news. Look — I'd be happy to chip
in. Did you bring extra posters or something? I
could tack 'em up at the grocers.

                    KATHERINE
It's not about canvassing...

                    KATHERINE pulls DAISY's actor
                    photograph out of her purse.

                    DAISY
Oh, *she's* cute.

                    KATHERINE
Is this you?

                        DAISY
Partially.

                        KATHERINE
How do you mean?

                        DAISY
That's the old me.

                        KATHERINE
Did you used to be an actress?

                        DAISY
No, I used to be a waitress.
          (Pause, a wink)
I suppose I know how you got my address. Only three
people in the world have that mug shot. The other
ninety-seven copies are in a box in my closet. I gave
one to my mother. A lousy ex-boyfriend stole the
second. That's not all he took. And he's married. I
doubt you asked his chick-a-dee for a peek-a-boo.

                        KATHERINE
Why didn't you tell me on Sunday that you were an
actress?

                        DAISY
Because I'm not. I'm a girl with a pretty picture.

                        ZOEY
In a film agent's drawer!

                        ZOEY regrets saying this.

                        DAISY
Ah. It's the copy I gave John Harbour.

                        KATHERINE
I wish you had told me you were an actress.

                        DAISY
It doesn't matter.

KATHERINE

It's a connection. Did Sienna go on auditions with you?

DAISY

Sometimes.

KATHERINE

Do the police know this?

DAISY

I'm not so proud of my auditions.

KATHERINE

Every person Sienna had contact with is important to finding her. Look, the last time we saw Sienna she did something.

ZOEY

She did a trick.

KATHERINE

Yes, she did this magic trick. She, she put her hand out and there was light - this bright white light from the palm of her hand. And-

DAISY

Not much of a trick.

KATHERINE

It wasn't the- I mean, it looked easy. It was just light. But there was no source. It was like it came from *inside* of my daughter. It was like it was *hers*... And she did it like a kid putting on a show. She did it without any sense, like she was stripped there naked and didn't realize it until she saw our faces. Please. Did Sienna know anyone who could have taught her this trick?

DAISY

I don't see what a silly trick has to do with-

KATHERINE

Please.

                    DAISY
We didn't know any magicians, if that's what you're
asking. We never auditioned for any magic shows or
variety hours or anything. If she were up for
someone's assistant or something, she would have told
me.
               (Thinking)
Wait a sec...

                    ZOEY
What? What?

                              DAISY goes towards her dressing
                              table. She combs through a
                              drawer.

                    DAISY
There was this one guy. He was off to the side during
this one audition. He chatted up Sienna pretty good.
I think he gave us a coupla cards. Here-

                              DAISY hands the card to KATHERINE.

                    KATHERINE
          (Reading)
"David Wolff, Master Technician." I don't understand.

                    DAISY
Guy who makes flying saucers fly and stuff. Blows
things up. Film effects.

                    KATHERINE
Yes. Yes. He sounds promising.

                    DAISY
I can't vouch for him or anything. Seemed a little
quiet. Cute. But a bore. Took more of an interest
in Sienna than me.

                    ZOEY
Did she ever see him again?

                             DAISY

I don't think so. I'm not sure. He never called our
apartment, so...

                           KATHERINE pockets the card.

                             KATHERINE

Thank you.

                           DAISY

You're welcome.

                             KATHERINE drifts, unsure of what
                             to say. <u>She spots a doll on a</u>
                             <u>shelf</u>. She approaches it but does
                             not touch it.

                               KATHERINE
                    (Lump in throat)
This is Sienna's.

                           DAISY

Uh-huh.

                           ZOEY

Is that Princess?

                            KATHERINE

I thought... I thought she threw this away. When she
was a girl.

                             KATHERINE strokes the doll. She
                             pulls the doll from the shelf.
                             She holds it. Slowly, she wraps
                             it in her arms. Finally, she puts
                             it back on the shelf.

                           DAISY

You can keep it if you want.

KATHERINE
No. It should be here for her when she gets back.

                    KATHERINE turns against the wall,
                    hiding.

                    ZOEY puts her hands on her mother.

ZOEY
Let's go, Mom. I think we're done.

DAISY
It must be nice to be loved.

ZOEY
Where're your parents?

DAISY
I'm an orphan. They died in a fire when I was three.

ZOEY
That doesn't mean you're not loved.

DAISY
Right. Not necessarily. But in this case it does.

                    KATHERINE hugs DAISY.

KATHERINE
I wish Sienna had introduced us. She was always so
secret about her Hollywood friends. But you've been
very nice.

DAISY
I try.

ZOEY
Thanks.

                    They open the door to leave.

                        ZOEY (Continued)
Oh. One more thing. Have you ever heard of a movie
called *Hunt Her, Kill Her*?

                        DAISY
You mean that horrid poster in John's office?

                        ZOEY
That's the one.

                        DAISY
Don't mention that. I just missed getting that part.
One of my many, many rejections.

                        KATHERINE
Did you know the girl who starred in the picture?

                        DAISY
I don't know if you could say "starred." It was
pretty low budget picture, far as I could tell. Bunch
of creepy men in a room looking at your legs. I doubt
they could afford a star. But I know what you mean.
Did I know her the same way I knew Sienna? No. She
was just some girl. Never saw her again.

                        KATHERINE
So she was a stranger?

                        DAISY
To me.

                        KATHERINE nods. She exits with
                        her daughter.

                        DAISY (Continued)
I'll call if something big comes up, okay?

                        DAISY shuts the door and resumes
                        dressing. She sits at the makeup
                        table.

                        From behind her, quietly, the
                        front door opens again...

Standing in the door is <u>a PERSON</u>
<u>wearing a trench coat, with a hat,</u>
<u>face covered by a mask</u>.

                    DAISY (Continued)
              (Over shoulder, joking)
Well I haven't heard anything *yet*!

She dabs powder on her nose.

The PERSON enters fully.

A SECOND PERSON appears in the
doorway — identical in stature and
dress (trench coat, hat, mask.)

<u>These two combined are known as</u>
<u>CARBON COPY</u>.

                    DAISY (Continued)
Change your mind on taking "Princess"?

DAISY turns and startles.

                    DAISY (Continued)
              (Panicked)
Please. Please.

<u>A fight breaks out</u>.

<u>DAISY is knocked unconscious</u>.

CARBON begins to arrange the
apartment...

COPY goes to the shelf and tugs
SIENNA's doll. COPY stares the
doll down, as if it were an alien
thing. In the end, COPY snaps the
doll's head before lazily tossing

the parts aside, then returns to
the work at hand.

CARBON pulls from a pocket a
hangman's noose and begins to
string it from the rafter of the
apartment.

They lift Daisy, reviving, towards
the dangling noose.

At last - she SCREAMS! It's
doubled and screeching through the
room.

Blackout.

Lights up again, low. Another
plan.

DAISY is dismembered behind the
sofa by CARBON, parts thrown as
the work is done.

Lights fade.

ACT I

SCENE 8

The LYMAN house.

REBECCA paces, and then sits.

KATHERINE and ZOEY enter.

REBECCA bolts from the chair and
to the door, a panicked look on
her face.

                    KATHERINE
          (Noticing)
What is it?

                    REBECCA
          (Rushed, in a whisper)
Go, go.

                    ZOEY
What's wrong?

                    REBECCA
You have to go. Quickly. He won't leave.

          SOUND: A toilet flushes.

                    KATHERINE
Who is it?

                    REBECCA
A policeman!

                    REBECCA shoves the two back
                    towards the door, but it's too
                    late, a man stands in the main
                    room.

                    He is stooped, in ratty brown suit
                    and Fedora hat.

This is DETECTIVE CHURCHYARD.

                    CHURCHYARD
Good afternoon.

                    He approaches the bar, fixes a
                    drink (very slowly) then points to
                    the sofa.

                    CHURCHYARD (Continued)
Please.

                    KATHERINE
You're in my house.

                    CHURCHYARD again points to the
                    sofa.

                    CHURCHYARD
Please.

                    REBECCA, ZOEY, and KATHERINE are
                    seated.

                    CHURCHYARD (Continued)
In the next ten minutes... I will know everything
about you. I will know how many lovers you had, which
of you was abused, all about your failed careers,
missed appointments. Your drinks of choice... or if
you're all teetotalers.
          (Eyes the bar)
See — I already know an answer and it's been ten
seconds. The Lymans' drink. Lots. Gin and whiskey,
it seems. No beer. No wine. Martinis for the
ladies, brown from the men. Have I got it?

                    KATHERINE
The bar is my husband's.

CHURCHYARD
Is? The present tense. Interesting.
          (Drinks)
Denial is common.

KATHERINE
My daughter tells us you're a policeman.

CHURCHYARD
Detective. As I said, in ten minutes... I'll know
everything.

KATHERINE
Do you have some information about my daughter?

CHURCHYARD
She's twenty-seven and lost a baby a month ago when
near term. She doesn't like you much and wishes you
behaved more like a mother than a cat-in-heat. She's
never seen you work. She knows she's not your
favorite and you've recently had a severe argument
that she regrets.

KATHERINE
          (To REBECCA)
How long was he here before we arrived?

CHURCHYARD
Five minutes — two of them lost to pissing.

KATHERINE
I doubt she told you all that.

CHURCHYARD
She didn't have to. I could tell. She's like one of
those magazines with large print and lots of pictures.
The kind you buy in the grocery line and read in the
toilet.

KATHERINE
You must not be that smart after all. My question: do
you have information? *That* question was about my
other daughter, Sienna.

                    CHURCHYARD
The one who is missing.

                    KATHERINE
Yes.

                    CHURCHYARD
I'm not here about her. I'm here about her agent.

                    KATHERINE
          (Smooth)
Is that the man who was at Connor's funeral? See, I'm
not in denial, Detective Churchyard.

                    CHURCHYARD
          (Indicating REBECCA)
She told you my name?

                    KATHERINE
There's a laundry tag hanging from your coat.

                         CHURCHYARD looks down. He snaps
                         the tag with his name from his
                         sleeve.

                    KATHERINE (Continued)
Is it possible, Detective, that in ten minutes I'll
know everything about you..?

                         CHURCHYARD smiles. He gulps his
                         drink, sets it down on the bar,
                         and pulls a chair in front of the
                         sofa.

                    CHURCHYARD
You think you're a clever girl.

                    KATHERINE
I'm not a girl. I'm a woman. And I'm not trying to
be clever.

                              ZOEY
                    (Injecting, nervous)
          Really, she's not that smart.

                              KATHERINE quickly smacks ZOEY's
                              leg. ZOEY gives a slight "ow."

                              CHURCHYARD
          Well... I suppose I know who is abused.

                              KATHERINE
          What do you want?

                              CHURCHYARD
          Haven't you guessed?

                              KATHERINE
          I have no idea.

                              CHURCHYARD
          Yes. You. Do.

                              Long pause.

                              KATHERINE
          Is this a staring contest? Or are you going to say
          something?

                              CHURCHYARD
          John Harbour, your daughter's agent, was found this
          morning, murdered. Someone had beaten him to death in
          his West Hollywood office. Probably with a club or a
          pipe. Though his telephone is missing, so there's a
          case for that.

                              KATHERINE
                    (Giving away nothing)
          Wow. That's terrible.

CHURCHYARD

I've seen your films. Yes, that's right. Six films
in eight years and then you stopped. It's a shame
they don't cast you anymore. I don't think you've
gotten ugly or anything. In fact... Yeah, if I was
making a movie, you'd be on my list. Your husband was
in the business, too, wasn't he?

KATHERINE

He was a set painter.

CHURCHYARD

This is a nice house for a set painter.

KATHERINE

The money is mine.

CHURCHYARD

I don't believe your contract with the studio could
have paid for all this. I suppose I know how many
lovers you had, then.

CHURCHYARD makes a checkmark in
the air with his finger, marks the
time sarcastically.

KATHERINE

You know exactly nothing. If you were any good at
detecting, you'd tell me where Sienna has gone.

CHURCHYARD

What makes you think I don't know already?

KATHERINE slaps CHURCHYARD.

REBECCA

Mother!

CHURCHYARD
(Holding cheek, smiles)
No worries, girls. I'm not going to bring your mother
up on assaulting a policeman.

CHURCHYARD stands, goes to the
bar, and fixes another drink.
Deliberately, he over-pours his
whiskey, splashing the bar,
winking as he does so.

                    CHURCHYARD
Ooops.

                    KATHERINE
You must go.

                    CHURCHYARD
Don't you want to hear it? You wouldn't want this
fountain of knowledge to dry up, would you?

                    KATHERINE
You've told us nothing.

                    CHURCHYARD
          (Sly)
So you knew about Mr. Harbour's murder, then?

                    KATHERINE
Well... No. That was news.

                    CHURCHYARD
I'll tell you what else is news. You girls are out of
your depths. You're going to get swept into the
Pacific if you're not careful. I can already tell
there's a curse. Missing daughter, dead husband, dead
baby... and now another body turns up. Death is
trying to get in your panties. I wouldn't want to be
within three miles of you.

                    ZOEY
That's fine by us.

                    CHURCHYARD
So bubble gum girl speaks. Good for you. I love a
mix of false courage and desperation. Makes the game
more interesting.

                    REBECCA
Isn't your ten minutes up?

CHURCHYARD

So the baby comment riles you, huh? The Lyman's have
rallied for another round, another set of blows...
another... go with... gloves off... Well... Here's to
fool's courage...

> CHURCHYARD finishes this latest
> drink.

CHURCHYARD (Continued)

May I use your telephone?

KATHERINE

No you may not.

> CHURCHYARD crosses to the phone.
> He lifts the receiver, and then
> thinks. He bends. He puts the
> heavy receiver to the top of his
> head, as if administering an
> imaginary, slow motion blow. He
> knows the three are watching him
> assess this possibility. He
> smiles.

CHURCHYARD

These things are heavy!

KATHERINE

Are you going to make a call or not?

> CHURCHYARD hangs up.

CHURCHYARD

I'll do it from the corner.

KATHERINE

If you're trying to intimidate us, or if you think we
killed Mr. Harbour-

                        CHURCHYARD
You know what I think?

                        CHURCHYARD crosses to KATHERINE,
                        moves close to her face.

                        CHURCHYARD (Continued)
You know what I *know*? That you are a goddamned liar.

                        He waits for the slap. When it
                        doesn't come, he backs away.

                        CHURCHYARD (Continued)
You all are. And I'll be back when I can prove it.

                        CHURCHYARD goes to the door, tips
                        his Fedora.

                        CHURCHYARD (Continued)
Have a super swell day.

                        He exits.

                        The three let out an audible
                        breath.

                        KATHERINE
That man was no policeman.

                        Curtain.

ACT II

SCENE 1

Lights rise on <u>TWO VAMPIRES,</u>
<u>females scantily clad in black.</u>
It is a scene of seduction. They
kiss on a bed before the audience.

This ends with dismemberment, a
geyser of blood, and a freeze
frame.

Lights out.

Lights on.

From the audience, ARCHIE ANDERS
storms the stage. He looks at the
blank screen before him. He
touches it, thinks, and then
paces.

A woman appears in darkness --
KATHERINE, barely seen.

                    KATHERINE
People aren't going to like it.

                    ARCHIE
Why does it have to be liked?

                    KATHERINE
Because if no one likes it, it won't last.

                    ARCHIE
Then how do you explain wars?

          KATHERINE comes forward.

                    KATHERINE
Too smart for me, Archie Anders. Your pretty
secretary told me to come on in.

                    ARCHIE
She *is* pretty, isn't she?

                              ARCHIE gives KATHERINE an embrace,
                              lets it linger.

                    ARCHIE (Continued)
She's too young.

                    KATHERINE
Trouble.

                    ARCHIE
Wants to be an actress.

                    KATHERINE
Double trouble.

                    ARCHIE
She recently got picked up for some small potatoes
deal. Stays out late at night and comes in with bags
under her eyes.

                    KATHERINE
Ah, youth. Wasted.

                    ARCHIE
You're got a secret. I can tell. It's keeping you
preserved. What kind of witchcraft are you involved
with?

                    KATHERINE
Do you make her run the projector?

                    ARCHIE
I have to. I'm getting arthritis. It's the Devil.
Ol' Archie Anders isn't want he used to be. I can
barely smack around the actors anymore.

                    KATHERINE
Your hands don't seem to be an issue tonight.

                              ARCHIE breaks.

ARCHIE

I thought I'd never see you again. You cut me off at the knees, you know.

KATHERINE

You can take it. You're a big boy.

ARCHIE

How's Connor?

KATHERINE

Connor died. Seven days ago.

ARCHIE

Holy crap. I'm sorry, Katherine. I liked him.

KATHERINE

So did I. It just took me a little long to realize it.

ARCHIE

One of the best painters I ever had. What happened?

KATHERINE

His heart.

ARCHIE

Shame. How are the girls taking it?

KATHERINE

The girls, the girls. My life isn't as perfect as it looks to the neighbors. I've lost control of everything. You know what being lost in the woods must be to a blind person? A nightmare. A complete and total nightmare.
          (Pause)
I need someone I can trust.

ARCHIE

Don't you trust your daughters?

KATHERINE

I do. But I've realized in the past few weeks that
          (MORE)

                         KATHERINE (Continued)
we're all very weak. In different ways. It's kind of
a shock. I always thought I was good at things. Now
I know I'm not. The only thing left for me is to
protect my children. It's the only thing that really
matters.

                         ARCHIE
I'm happy to do any-

                         KATHERINE
I'm in a lot of trouble, Archie. Sienna's been
missing for more than a month. And I've lost my
memory.

                         ARCHIE
What are you talking about?

                         KATHERINE
I can't remember anything before last Sunday. I only
remember the last time I saw Sienna. I can't even
remember Connor's funeral.

                              ARCHIE holds up a finger. He goes
                              to a telephone Rolodex, pulls a
                              card, and hands it to KATHERINE.

                         ARCHIE
Doctor Hans Renner. Best headshrinker in town. Just
have him send me the bills, care of the production
office. Guy's a genius. Got me to quit smoking, if
you can believe that.

                         KATHERINE
I need help, but not that kind. I need information.

                         ARCHIE
Sit down.

                         They are seated.

                         ARCHIE (Continued)
You look like you're gonna cry.

                    KATHERINE
I forgot: you hate it when women cry.

                    ARCHIE
That's because it's usually my fault.

                    KATHERINE
          (Smiles)
Not this time.

                    ARCHIE
Why come to me?

                    KATHERINE
You know people.

                    ARCHIE
I used to. I made some great movies, didn't I?

                    KATHERINE
You did. You do.

                    ARCHIE
I bet you haven't seen my last few pictures. Limited
releases. Exploitation, they call them in the trades,
because of the content. But they're wrong. It's not
the content that's exploitive. It's what they're
doing to my name. I used to be top tier. Be glad you
haven't sunk to this. You got out with your dignity
intact.

                    KATHERINE
All actresses have to choose. You have talent and
push through, grow old. Or you find a way into the
bed of someone with power who can take care of you
when the carousel stops. Those are the only choices.

                    ARCHIE
Katherine, I could have made you a star, if you'd have
let me.

                    KATHERINE
Don't remind me of your silly promises.

ARCHIE

You thought I was up to no good, but it's not true,
doll. I wanted to do right by you. I saw you in that
little part and I thought, "Wow." It was greatness,
wasn't it? That's what I saw.

KATHERINE

There wasn't anything great about me.

ARCHIE

Bullshit. There was plenty great about you.
          (Laugh)
The way you kissed, for one...

KATHERINE

Please. It's embarrassing.

ARCHIE

So now you're here. You came alone.

KATHERINE

I did. No one knows, Archie. No one knows.

ARCHIE

No one suspected? All those years.

KATHERINE

They suspected. But no one knew.

ARCHIE

Then why'd we stop?

KATHERINE

Two years ago Sienna told me she wanted to be an
actress. So I found myself trying to talk her out of
it.

ARCHIE

I saw that southern picture. I thought she was real
good. I hoped to give you a call after its run, see
what she was doing next.

KATHERINE

Put her in exploitation?

ARCHIE

No, no, see you got it wr-

KATHERINE

Did she look like me?

ARCHIE

Absolutely.
          (Pause)
So why are you alone? Katherine...

KATHERINE

Rebecca and Zoey are out looking for Sienna tonight.
Checking the places where only the young can go
without glares. I, I snuck away. If they saw me with
you, it'd be undone. They'd know. They're not dumb.
They know I've not been faithful, but if they knew it
was you and just you... That's another matter.
Children don't like to know that a mother could love
two men.
          (Pause)
Do you know a movie called *Hunt Her, Kill Her*?

ARCHIE

Oh, why you want to go talking about that?

KATHERINE

Have you heard of it?

ARCHIE

Yes. But I wish I hadn't.

ARCHIE stands, uncomfortable.

KATHERINE

Is it exploitation film like the ones you've been
making?

ARCHIE

I've never made *anything* like that one.

KATHERINE

But you've seen it?

ARCHIE

No. No, I haven't. Wouldn't want to. Listen, is
this about Sienna?

KATHERINE
The woman who starred in that movie had the same agent
as Sienna.

ARCHIE
Christ, Katherine. It's one of those movies that...
is really, *really* underground. Doesn't play in
theaters. Gets shown in basements. Sometimes in
private estates owned by rich weirdos from old
Hollywood who let all that glitter go to their heads.
It's extreme.

KATHERINE
How extreme?

ARCHIE
Like I said, I haven't seen it.

KATHERINE
Can you get a copy of it?

ARCHIE
Oh, God, come on, Katherine. You don't want to watch
that stuff.

KATHERINE
Do you know the people who made it?

ARCHIE
It's all fake names.

KATHERINE
So you've looked?

ARCHIE
Movies like that... they come up in conversations.

KATHERINE
Conversations with whom?

ARCHIE
Exploitation films attract... all kinds of people.
New talent, kids just wanting a break, but there's
also a... fringe element. I don't ride that far out.
I make women gladiator films with tits and blood. I
(MORE)

ARCHIE (Continued)

make titles like *The Grave Zombies* and *Castle Von Death*. I stay clear of *Hunt Her, Kill Her.* That's a different league.

KATHERINE

Is it pornography?

ARCHIE

Listen, Katherine. I don't want to scare you.

KATHERINE

I want to see it.

ARCHIE paces.

ARCHIE

This is a helluva favor.
          (Thinking)
Okay, okay. I, I might have a connection. Let me see what I can do. But it's a bad idea. A bad idea. You escaped it; you don't know what this town is like. And when you were in front of the cameras, you saw the good years. You missed what the last ten years have been like.

KATHERINE

There was reefer back then, too, you know.

ARCHIE

I'm not talking about-. This town's got a side that's lies just beyond the disappointments. A blackness. Horrors that are like deep cuts in the skin. People you wouldn't want to know in a million years. Have you heard about Carbon Copy? No? They've been around since Christmas. Two thugs in trench coats and hats -- right out of a Cagney film. Twins or something wearing Halloween masks. Done some killings around town. Brutal. Massacres. You don't hear it on the news because it's like reporting on the Flying Dutchman. Rumors and gossip. But everyone knows they're out there. And there are cults and there are maniacs and there are sects of all kinds of unholy violence-

                        KATHERINE
You're scaring me.

                        ARCHIE
Good. You should stay away.

                    KATHERINE stands.

                        KATHERINE
I have to find Sienna. I have to find out what
happened.

                        ARCHIE
Okay. Aside from this big favor, and believe me, it's
a big one, you got any easy requests?

                        KATHERINE
Do you know any special effects people?

                        ARCHIE
Some.

                        KATHERINE
David Wolff?

                        ARCHIE
No.

                        KATHERINE
Someone taught Sienna a magic trick.

                        ARCHIE
A disappearing act?

                    KATHERINE goes for the door.

                        KATHERINE
Yes. Something like that. A trick with light. This
trick is connected to her disappearance. I know it.
        (Pause)
Do you know any magic, Archie?

ARCHIE shakes his head sadly.

KATHERINE (Continued)

You have my number.

ARCHIE nods.

Blackout.

ACT II

SCENE 2

Dark.

A bare apartment, razor of light.

SOUND: Flies buzzing.

Enter ZOEY through a window.

Once inside, she helps REBECCA
over the ledge.

ZOEY
(Whisper)
It smells awful. I can't see anything.

REBECCA
(Whisper)
Find the switch.

ZOEY gropes the wall.

ZOEY
(Whisper)
Found it.

Pause.

REBECCA
(Whisper)
Well, turn on the lights!

ZOEY
(Whisper)
The switch must be broken. Get the flashlight.

REBECCA pulls a flashlight from
her bag.

                        ZOEY (Continued)
              (Whisper)
      I told you we'd need it.

                        REBECCA
              (Whisper)
      This is stupid, I feel like a robber.

                        REBECCA lights the flashlight and
                        scans the room.

                        She quickly settles on:

                        A dead body, tied to a chair,
                        covered in blood.

                        The two scream.

                        ZOEY
              (Whisper)
      Oh my God, oh my God, oh my God.

                        REBECCA
              (Whisper)
      Is that him?

                        REBECCA approaches the body,
                        shines the light.

                        ZOEY
      Look at his throat.

                        They back away.

                        REBECCA
      So much for David Wolff.

                        ZOEY
      We're leaving.

She backs away, trips.

When Rebecca reaches for her,
CARBON leaps from behind the sofa
and snatches ZOEY.

                    REBECCA
            (Screaming)
Zoey! Zoey!

The flashlight follows as ZOEY is
dragged behind the sofa.

The light goes out then comes back
on.

A bruising fight erupts in the
dark.

REBECCA makes it to the window.

COPY grabs REBECCA's face to stop
her call for help.

In the struggle, REBECCA pulls off
COPY's mask. Though REBECCA
doesn't see the face, it is
clearly SIENNA.

SIENNA is zombie-like,
unmistakably her, but without
emotion.

COPY/SIENNA chokes REBECCA, who at
last gets free. She makes it to
the door, throws it open, and
runs.

COPY/SIENNA replaces her mask.

ZOEY has fallen behind the sofa,
her legs showing, but not moving.

CARBON stands up.

CARBON COPY looks to each other.

Lights fade.

ACT II

SCENE 3

KATHERINE is asleep, wrapped in a robe.

REBECCA enters, winded, goes straight to her mother, weeping.

KATHERINE holds her daughter.

                    KATHERINE
It's okay. It's okay. Rebecca, it's okay.

                    REBECCA
          (Through tears)
No, it's not. It's not.

                    KATHERINE
Where's Zoey?
          (Pause)
Where's Zoey?

                    KATHERINE pulls REBECCA away. She
                    sees the cuts on her daughter's
                    face from the struggle.

                    REBECCA
We went to David Wolff's house.

                    KATHERINE
You stupid girls.

                    REBECCA
Mom. Mom. It was awful.

                    KATHERINE
Tell me what happened.

                    REBECCA
He was dead, Mom. Someone had killed him. With a
knife. He was tied in a chair. And then we were
attacked. These two... people. Wearing these masks,
and-

                    KATHERINE
Oh, Lord, no-

                    RECECCA
They got Zoey. It was dark. I ran away. She was on
the floor. I don't know if she was all right. I left
her. I left her. Oh, God, Mom. I ran away.

                    KATHERINE
          (Shaking REBECCA)
Was she alive?

                    REBECCA
I don't know. I don't know.

                    KATHERINE
You should have helped her?

                    REBECCA
I had to get away! Mom, I had to.

                    KATHERINE
We've got to... We've got to phone the police.

                    REBECCA
Okay, okay.

                    KATHERINE stands and goes for the
                    phone.

                    SOUND: Knocks at the door.

                    The two freeze.

                    Knocks.

                    Turning to pounding.

                    KATHERINE
          (In a whisper)
Did they follow you?

REBECCA
            (Mouthing)
I don't know.

            REBECCA silently sobs.

            KATHERINE moves towards the door.

            REBECCA tries to warn her away,
            but is shushed.

CHURCHYARD
            (Through door, singsong)
Mrs. Lyman! It's Detective Churchyard.

            Long pause.

CHURCHYARD (Continued)
            (Through door)
I know you're in there, Mrs. Lyman.
            (Pause)
I brought a present for you.
            (Pause)
I know you're gonna like it.

KATHERINE
Go away!

CHURCHYARD
            (Through door)
You *are* there, Mrs. Lyman. I'm a good detective.
Don't you want to see my present?

KATHERINE
I said go away!

CHURCHYARD
            (Through door)
If now's a bad time, I could just leave it at the
door.

KATHERINE
I don't want *anything* from you.

CHURCHYARD
(Through door)
That's too bad, Mrs. Lyman. I thought you'd enjoy my
present. As a matter of fact, I *know* you'll enjoy it.

KATHERINE
I'm calling the police!

CHURCHYARD
(Through door)
That's funny. We're already here.

KATHERINE
You're not the police.

CHURCHYARD
(Through door)
I'm not? News to me, Mrs. Lyman. News. To. Me.
(Pause)
I'll just leave it by the door. Goodnight, Mrs.
Lyman. And goodnight, Rebecca. Take care of that
pretty ass.

SOUND: Footsteps. Long pause.

KATHERINE peers outside.

KATHERINE
(Soft)
I think he's gone.

REBECCA
Call the police.

KATHERINE puts her hand on the
door.

KATHERINE
I will.

                    REBECCA
Now, Mother, now!

                    KATHERINE opens the door.

                    She sees something on the ground,
                    reaches down slowly, embraces it,
                    rises with an object clutched in
                    her arms, hidden until she
                    turns...

                    It is the telephone she used to
                    kill JOHN HARBOUR. She quickly
                    pulls inside and bolts the door.

                    KATHERINE
The telephone.

                    REBECCA
He knows, he knows!

                    KATHERINE
Maybe it's a different—

                    REBECCA
Look at the dent.

                    KATHERINE throws down the phone.

                    KATHERINE
I can't call the police.

                    REBECCA
Please, Mother. You've *got* to. Zoey! Please,
Mother!

                    KATHERINE stares at the murder
                    weapon. She can't take her eyes
                    from it.

                    KATHERINE
How did he find this? We threw it off the pier.

                    REBECCA
I don't know! We have to call THE POLICE!

                    REBECCA stands.

                    REBECCA (Continued)
I'll call them!

                    KATHERINE moves between the
                    house's phone and her daughter.

                    KATHERINE
Just wait, just wait.

                    REBECCA
Mom, it's Zoey! It's Zoey!

                    REBECCA tries to barrel past her
                    KATHERINE, who struggles with her.

                    REBECCA (Continued)
You don't think I couldn't claw my way through you?
Are you going to kill me with that phone, too? I'm
CALLING the POLICE! We need HELP! We need
HEEEELLLLLLLLP!

                    REBECCA's scream startles
                    KATHERINE out of something.

                    KATHERINE
You're right. We should, we should...

                    REBECCA
Get out of my way.

REBECCA rushes to the phone. Just
as she's about to pick up the
receiver, it rings.

The two women stare it down.

REBECCA grabs it.

                    ARCHIE
          (Over phone)
Hello? Is anyone there?
          (Pause)
Katherine? It's Archie Anders. Hello?

REBECCA turns, gives her mother a
look of supreme disappointment
before handing the phone over.

                    REBECCA
I knew it. He was one of them.

                    KATHERINE
You're wrong.

                    REBECCA
I'm not.

KATHERINE takes the phone.

                    KATHERINE
          (Into phone)
Archie.

                    ARCHIE
          (Over phone)
Katherine! Good. I've learned something tonight. I
wanted to tell you right away.

                    KATHERINE
David Wolff's dead.

                    ARCHIE

(Over phone)
He is? That's the effects man you mentioned? How do
you know?

                    KATHERINE
I read it.

                    ARCHIE
          (Over phone)
Oh. Well, it's not that. You mentioned a magic
trick. I've seen something, Katherine. You have to
see it, too. It's that movie. *Hunt Her, Kill Her.*
I've got it. I think you should come over right away.
There's something in this film you should see. But I
have to have the print back by midnight or I'm a dead
man. You must hurry, Katherine.

                    KATHERINE
Tell me, Archie. Tell me now.

                    ARCHIE
          (Over phone)
Can't. You have to see it. Hurry or you'll miss it.

          SOUND: Click.

          KATHERINE looks to REBECCA.

                    KATHERINE
Can you drive?

                    REBECCA
What?

                    KATHERINE
Archie's found the film.

                    REBECCA
What film?

                    KATHERINE

Hunt Her, Kill Her. I asked him to find it. It's an underground film. Something we're not supposed to see. He has it for just another two hours.

> KATHERINE

We can't go see a MOVIE!

> KATHERINE

He mentioned magic.
>   (Compelling)
You *know* it, Rebecca. You *have* to know this. Everything bad started with Sienna's trick.

> REBECCA

We need the police. Not a film director.

> KATHERINE

I trust Archie.

> REBECCA

He doesn't know about Zoey. She comes first.

> KATHERINE

The police can't help Zoey. Only we can save her. If it's magic, then there's a chance. We have to find the source.

>   REBECCA breaks. She goes wild,
>   breaking things, throwing things.

> KATHERINE

We're wasting time, Rebecca.

> REBECCA

Everything we do just gets us in deeper.

> KATHERINE

You're right.

> REBECCA

I'm so mad at you. At Sienna. At Zoey. At Dad. Everyone leaves.

KATHERINE

I'm here.

REBECCA

You screwed around.

KATHERINE

I did. But I loved your father. I gave Archie up two
years ago because I realized that. I love all of you
so very much. And I've let all these terrible things
happen.

KATHERINE turns away, crying.

REBECCA considers.

REBECCA

One stop... then the police station.

KATHERINE nods, wipes her eyes.

KATHERINE

We don't have a pistol, do we?

REBECCA

You killed a man with a *phone*, Mom. I think we'll be
okay.

Lights fade.

ACT II

SCENE 4

ARCHIE ANDERS' home.

ARCHIE, KATHERINE, and REBECCA sit
in dim lights.

ARCHIE
Before I run this, I want to be sure.

KATHERINE
I'm sure. How long is it?

ARCHIE
Forty-one minutes. Short, but effective. And
disturbing. Black and white. Parts are violent.
          (Pause)
I'm going to run it on from the booth. But I won't
come back into the room. I don't want to see it a
second time.

                    ARCHIE exits. After a moment, the
                    film begins...

                    The scene accelerates -- collages
                    of sound, flickers, and images.
                    Bright red lights overlap black
                    and white strobes.

                    KATHERINE and REBECCA are
                    transfixed.

                    At a point, Rebecca shouts over
                    the screams emanating from the
                    film's soundtrack:

                    REBECCA
Sienna! It's her...

                    KATHERINE can only nod.

The film turns into blaring white
light that holds the room in a
noisy haze, which is overtaken by
red.

The film whirls to climax then
stops.

SOUND: Clop, clop, clop of a
finished film reel slapping the
projector's feeder, slowing to
end.

ARCHIE returns, carrying a film
can.

                    KATHERINE
          (Soft)
Did you see it?

                    REBECCA
I did.

                    KATHERINE
That woman on the poster does the trick in the film.
Sienna's not in the scene. She knew the start of it,
but not the result.

                    REBECCA
Did you see what it did to those people? It cut them
all into little pieces.

                    KATHERINE
Sienna had no idea what she did in our living room
that day. If she had let it continue, it would have
killed us all.

                    ARCHIE
Like a child with a new toy.

                    KATHERINE
In the film, it's not *really* her.

                    ARCHIE
Of course it's her. That's why I wanted you to see
it.

REBECCA
Mom's right. It's not her. She's... under a spell.

KATHERINE
Like *I* was when I lost my memory.

ARCHIE
Is it witchcraft? Possibly. It's a snuff film for
certain. Films are tricks. Everything about them is
a lie. People die, people live, but not really. It's
all fake. But there's one thing you can't fake: the
look on those people's faces when they died. That's
for real. I know it in my gut. People have died.
          (Pause)
The two in the trench coats, in that one decapitation
scene...

KATHERINE
Carbon Copy.

ARCHIE
That's right. Not a myth. Characters in a snuff film
brought to life.

KATHERINE
I feel like I've just watched one of those accident
films they show you in driver's school, to frighten
you. Sienna's not a murderer. She's an actress. She
wants to be a film star.

ARCHIE
Katherine. Stay away from... from, whatever this is.
This thing that Sienna's involved with, it's eaten her
alive. No one in his or her right mind would do those
things and then come to a family gathering. She's
lost.

KATHERINE
Do you know what you're saying? This is my *daughter*.

ARCHIE
I know what I'm saying.

KATHERINE
I'm her mother. I'm her mother. The spell can be
broken.

ARCHIE

It's too dangerous.

REBECCA

We were going to go to the police.

ARCHIE

The police?

REBECCA

Zoey's been taken by those two in the coats.

ARCHIE

What? Why didn't you tell me this?

KATHERINE

There's a man who is following us. He says he's with
the police. We don't trust him. He may be dangerous.
We decided to come her first and see the film.

ARCHIE

But if they took your youngest child-

KATHERINE

She may even be dead.
          (Pause)
Who gave you this film?

ARCHIE

A friend of a friend of a friend of a friend. I don't
directly know the man. Runs a prop shop in Los Feliz.
If you want me to tell the police about him, I will.
I will do *anything* to help you, Katherine. If you
want to go to the police from here, I understand. But
I must return the film tonight. I'm be through if I
don't.

KATHERINE

We're not splitting up. I can't lose anyone else.

REBECCA

Turn the film over to the police.

                    ARCHIE
If I do, I'd be jeopardizing everyone who helped me
find it in the first place. And we might need those
sources. There may be more films out there. This
prop man -- he's established. He's not going
anywhere. He's probably just a middleman anyhow. But
if he's important, the police can locate him later
this morning. Please... I have to be there before
midnight. Let's go. My car is outside.

                    Lights out.

ACT II

SCENE 5

A warehouse.

Crates, racks of clothes.

<u>SOUND</u>: The door rattles with
pounding.

No answer.

The door opens. An arm shows.

Enter ARCHIE ANDERS clutching the
film. Behind him are KATHERINE
and REBECCA.

          ARCHIE
Hello...
      (No answer)
I'm back. I've brought the film.

          ARCHIE sets the film down on a
          crate.

          ARCHIE (Continued)
I'm leaving it here. Okay? Thanks for the loan.
      (Turning to the women)
Come on...

          A <u>MAN</u> steps from behind one of the
          costume racks and blocks the exit.
          He wears the <u>same mask</u> as CARBON
          COPY.

          The women startle.

                              ARCHIE (Continued)
          (Making light)
Okay. I'm impressed with your props and costumes.
But my friends and I really have to leave.
          (No answer)
We have to leave.

                         Slowly, THE MAN removes the mask.

                         It is CHURCHYARD.

                              ARCHIE
Funny joke. There's your film. Thanks for the loan.

                              KATHERINE
No, Archie, not him!

                         CHURCHYARD takes his hand from his
                         side. He holds a pistol.

                              ARCHIE
Come on, I've had enough of the props, buster.

                         CHURCHYARD waves his hand over the
                         gun.

                              CHURCHYARD
          (Sarcastically)
Abraaaaacabraaaaaa...

                         CHURCHYARD shoots ARCHIE in the
                         leg and he goes down. KATHERINE
                         dives to help him.

                              KATHERINE
No!

                    ARCHIE
Jesus Christ!

                    KATHERINE
Leave us alone!

                    CHURCHYARD
You were right, Mrs. Lyman. I'm not a policeman. But
I'm one helluva actor. And I've made some real
inroads into other skills popular in this town. I'm
an auteur. Couple underground classics. But I've got
a good feeling about this next one. Real potential at
the box office. Smiles for the cameras, girls...

                              From behind crates, CARBON
                              appears, wielding a film camera.
                              COPY is alongside, holding a boom
                              microphone.

                    CHURCHYARD (Continued)
It's a little tough to work unscripted, but it yields
spectacular results. I like my climaxes bloody. Get
the audiences worked into a nice frenzy. And you know
what else works magic in the last reel?

                              CHURCHYARD shoves aside a costume
                              rack and reveals ZOEY tied up and
                              gagged. ZOEY struggles through
                              her bindings.

                    CHURCHYARD (Continued)
          (Dry)
Surprise...
          (To CARBON)
Get in close. Real close.

                              CARBON puts the camera's lens
                              tight to KATHERINE's eye.

                    CHURCHYARD (Continued)
I like to see this: real emotion. You can't get that
from an actor. Not usually. Not unless they're
pushed. But cliffs aren't very cinematic. Oh. Mrs.
Lyman. Mrs. Ly... *man*. You used to be pretty. In
fifteen minutes, that, that porcelain grace, that,
that film star shine, that glow which you have passed
down through your drowning gene pool, will be forever
scarred. You will have to watch your children lose
their beauty. That will be hard for you.

                    KATHERINE
You're the Devil!

                    CHURCHYARD
Not true. But we do run in the same social circles.
          (To CARBON)
Get it all on film. We can shoot cutaways later. I
want... her face. The mother will tell the story.

                              CHURCHYARD crosses to a crate. He
                              opens it. He pulls out a short
                              sword. Then another. Then
                              another, slightly longer.

                    CHURCHYARD (Continued)
Which one of these would have the best effect on an
audience? Or...
          (Turns to ZOEY)
...a young girl's cheek.

                    REBECCA
It's not real!

                    CHURCHYARD
Oh, yes. Everything in my films is real. Even the
magic. I could do card tricks all day. But I prefer
things a bit more black.

                              CHURCHYARD, with gun and sword,
                              crosses to ZOEY. His hands are
                              full so he must put down the
                              pistol to cut the tape covering
                              her mouth.

It that moment, KATHERINE goes
wild and attacks him.

A fight breaks out:

The masked CARBON COPY, armed with
boom microphone and camera,

CHURCHYARD's gun firing,

ARCHIE crawling on the floor,

KATHERINE, REBECCA, ZOEY, and
CHURCHYARD...

It is chaos, with weapons and
props used viscously.

The lights go out — the fight
continues in the dark, they
flicker back on.

CARBON is killed.

COPY drops the boom and picks up
the camera.

In retaliation, CHURCHYARD shoots
REBECCA.

                KATHERINE

No!

CHURCHYARD begins to do a magic
trick with his hand, the power
rising and rising - the amplified
version of SIENNA's trick.

KATHERINE cuts off CHURCHYARD's
hand with a sword to a gush of
blood. He screams and collapses.
KATHERINE, short sword in one
hand, pistol aimed, shoots
CHURCHYARD dead.

At last, she turns to COPY, who
films it all, mask still on.

The film runs out of the camera
and it stops. COPY looks at the
camera dumbly, at last setting it
aside. COPY reaches in a trench
coat pocket.

KATHERINE fires and COPY falls.

Five bodies are now on the floor.

KATHERINE cuts ZOEY loose.

ARCHIE crawls to CARBON and takes
of the mask.

                    ARCHIE
Oh, Christ...

                    KATHERINE
What?

                    ARCHIE
It's my secretary.

KATHERINE bends to REBECCA, who is
bleeding, but alive. She takes
ZOEY's hand and folds it into
REBECCA's, for comfort.

Slowly, she approaches COPY. She
removes the mask and immediately
and despairingly begins to weep.

It's SIENNA.

                    KATHERINE
No, no. Sienna. I'm sorry, I'm sorry, I'm so sorry.

                    SIENNA
          (Weakly)

It's okay.

                    KATHERINE
We're going to get help. We're gonna get help.

                    SIENNA
Okay.

                    KATHERINE
I can't lose you.

                    SIENNA
Stay with me.

                    KATHERINE
Yes-

                    SIENNA
I've done bad things.

                    KATHERINE
It's all right. I saved you.

                    SIENNA
You did?

                    KATHERINE
Of course. I've saved you.

          SOUND: Distant sirens.

               KATHERINE (Continued)
See? They're coming. They're coming.

               ZOEY
What if they're not for us?

               KATHERINE
They are. They're for us. I know it.

               SIENNA
No. It's Hollywood.

Music and sound, the flickering of
a film running through a
projector.

Blackout.

Final curtain.

Special Thanks

The Casts and Crews of
Beautiful Women in Terrible Trouble

51Works, Groom Lake and esp. Davis Collins

Anderson Lawfer

Michael Driscoll

Polarity Ensemble Theatre, Chicago

Strawdog Theatre Company, Chicago

Richard Engling

John Klein

Glass City Films

Lisa, Liam, and Charlotte

Dario Argento

Past and Future Patrons of the Theatre Arts

Past and Future Producers of the Theatre Arts